TRADITIONAL INDIAN

BEAD & LEATHER

CRAFTS

BAGS, POUCHES AND CONTAINERS

BY

MONTE SMITH &
MICHELE VanSICKLE

Eagle's View Publishing
A WestWind Inc. Company
6756 North Fork Road
Liberty, UT 84310

Library of Congress Catalog Card Number: 86-83378
ISBN 0-943604-14-1

DEDICATION

**To Suzy - who is an inspiration and
means so much to each of us!**

TABLE OF CONTENTS

Projects

Techniques

Beading Patterns

Leather Patterns

INTRODUCTION

This is the second book in our series on Traditional Indian Crafts and is written in answer to numerous requests for "how to do it" books that would not only cover the basics of the traditional craft work of the American Indian, but would also present illustrated step-by-step instructions on how to do those crafts. With this in mind, the book is written with two objectives: First, it is directed to the person who simply wants to make a nice, attractive pouch or bag and desires a clear, concise guide to producing that particular item. And second, it will serve as a "primer" on the basics of traditional beadwork and leather crafts of Native Americans for the craftsperson who wants to understand these techniques and, thereby, be able to construct other items while using them.

How To Use This Book

(1) Many people will only want to construct two or three of the projects that are illustrated and explained in this book and, therefore, each project is written so that it is complete. In other words, there is no reason to read the entire book just to do one project. This means that there will be some repetition within the various projects, but we feel this is much better than constant references to other parts of the book.

At the same time, even if you are going to use this book for only one or two items, we strongly suggest that you take the time to read all of the information in this *Introduction*.

(2) Before beginning the construction of any item, be sure and read through all of the instructions for that project carefully so that you understand how each step fits into the completed item. Many of the projects have a number of *Hints* included at the end of the section and these should be helpful when doing the construction. If you want to personalize or make changes in the project, make some notes (there are pages provided for that purpose) and with these in mind, work step-by-step until the item is complete.

(3) Do not be afraid to change the projects or to "personalize" them. Many have been taken from museum pieces or pictures of Indian items, but if you want to reflect your personal preference or other Tribal influences, etc., be sure and do it.

Further, just because a project is shown with, for instance, a Lazy Stitch or with blue beads in the pattern there is no reason why it cannot be done in a Running Stitch or with green beads!

(4) In all cases, take your time and work with care. The patience you show while doing craftwork will show in the finished article.

(5) Each project includes a list of Materials Needed and these are the minimum amounts.

(6) All of the materials used in these instructions are available from a number of sources. If you do not find them at your local craft store it is certain that they may be obtained from any store specializing in Indian and mountain man craft supplies. If you do not have such a store in your area, there are a number of very good "mail order" sources.

(7) As with all craftwork, there are certain hazards associated with doing Indian crafts. Using needles, awls, scissors, etc. can be dangerous if you are not careful and it is strongly suggested that you plan your work and do it with the necessary caution and care.

Acknowledgments

All of the graphics and photography for this book were done by R. L. (Smitty) Smith whose talent is self evident. Special thanks to John Kramer for his additions to techniques using leather. The text has been read and proofed by Sue, Brad and Celia - their assistance is greatly appreciated.

LEATHER TECHNIQUES

(1) The very best leather for all of these projects is made from hides that have been brain tanned. If done properly, this leather is very soft throughout and is easy to cut and bead. Unfortunately, brain-tanned leather is fairly expensive and other leather, such as buckskin or light to medium-weight commercial leather will work fine.

In that each of these projects is fairly small it is probable that they can be done with one small hide. However, if it is necessary to use smaller pieces of leather, be sure and match them so that all of the leather has the same color, texture and consistency.

(2) Most available leather will have a rough (suede) and smooth side. If you are making a pouch that is made in the "Indian-style," the rough side should be on the outside. If, however, you are making settlement or "white man-style" goods, it would be more appropriate to have the smooth side out.

(3) To make a pattern from those used in this book, trace the patterns, using carbon paper, onto some heavy paper like butcher or brown wrapping paper as shown in **Figure 1**. Then trim the excess from your working pattern. A stiff pattern is easier to mark around when transfering the pattern to leather.

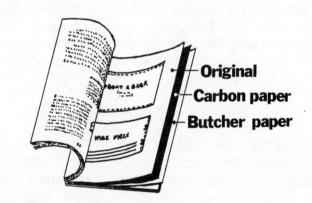

(4) To transfer the pattern to leather, you may use a charcoal pencil, soft lead pencil or dressmaker's chalk which comes in several colors. Usually it is best to mark the *Wrong Side*; that is, if the smooth side is going to be on the outside of the finished pouch, any marks should be made on the rough side of the leather. Further, it is also a good idea to test your marker on a scrap of the leather to see if it can be rubbed off later. For instance, a ball point pen makes great marks, but it is not removable and should be avoided.

(5) Whenever cutting light or medium-weight leathers, be sure and use a very sharp pair of scissors. If your cutting instrument is not sharp it will tear and stretch the leather instead of cutting it. For heavier leather a knife or razor edge may be used.

(6) Many otherwise perfect hides have skinning or skiving holes in them in inappropriate places, but a proper patch can add character to a finished pouch or bag. There are at least two methods of repairing holes in the leather (keep in mind that if you are going to adorn the finished item with beads or quills, it is better [easier] to do so if there are no holes or patches):

One method is to center the hole in an embroidery hoop and secure it with the retainer ring. Then cut a scrap of leather that is approximately one inch larger than the hole. Glue in place on the back side of the hole with rubber cement, making sure not to let any glue get on the *Right Side* of either the main piece or the patch. Allow to dry and then sew around the edge through both pieces with a running stitch (**Figure 2a**).

Or, you may cut out a piece of leather from scraps that is *almost* as big as the hole and then, using either a whip stitch or inside-out stitch, sew the piece into place. The leather will stretch into place making an even patch as shown in **Figure 2b**.

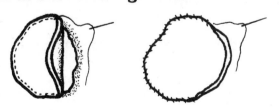

(7) After cutting out all of the pattern pieces, you may select pieces from the resulting scrap leather for thongs or laces. If you have a large enough piece, cut straight strips by one of the methods described below on how to make fringe. If you have small pieces or need very long thongs for lacing, trim one of the scraps into a rounded shape. Begin by cutting with a diagonal cut to the width you want and continue cutting around the outside of the piece while maintaining a uniform width. Round off any points or corners if they should develop. A six inch circle will produce many feet of lacing. (**Figure 3**)

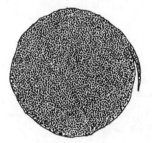

(8) Cotton, cotton-wrapped polyester, linen, sinew, artificial sinew (*see below*) and dental floss, among other products, can all be used for sewing leather. Prewaxing the thread by pulling it rapidly several times over a cake of beeswax will help prevent twisting and knotting of the thread.

(9) Imitation or Artificial Sinew is an ideal product for sewing leather. This product is made from endless man-made thread that has been impregnated with beeswax. It is extremely strong and is usually split into three or four threads for use in sewing by the method shown below in **Figure 4**.

7

(10) If sewing by machine, use cotton-wrapped polyester thread and leather machine needles purchased at a fabric store. Sewing leather requires a heavy duty sewing machine and it is not suggested that you use a regular machine for this purpose.

Most leather projects, however, are sewn by hand and this is easily done with a specialized needle called a Glover's Needle. These needles feature a triangular shaped point for going through leather, as pictured below, and it is suggested that you use the smallest needle that can easily be threaded with the desired thread. As with beading needles, *the larger the number the smaller the needle*; i.e., a size #8 is much smaller than a size #2.

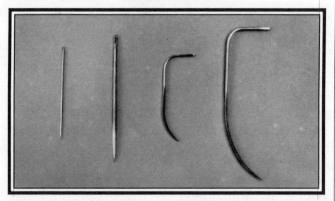

(11) At the beginning and end of each seam, the thread must be secured to prevent the sewing from coming undone with use. If you choose the whip stitch, hold a one inch length of thread in place within the seam and do the whip stitch over it. At the end of

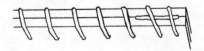

the seam, take the thread back through several stitches. With the running stitch, do a couple of double stitches at the beginning and ending of the seam. For machine sewing, back or double stitch at the beginning and end of the seam.

(12) Depending upon the leather that you have available, it is sometimes necessary or easier to sew it if you pre-punch the sewing holes. This may be done with a sharp square or triangular awl. This will not be necessary with brain-tanned leather, and with light-weight leather the awl may simply be pushed through the places where the holes should be. In heavier leather, or in spots where the leather was improperly tanned, it may be necessary to place the leather over a wood block (a stitching pad) and make the holes using a wood mallet.

Regardless of the method used, the holes should be slightly smaller than the thread being used and the holes must be evenly spaced. Stitches that are about 1/8" apart and evenly spaced are strong and attractive. This is a good rule of thumb even if you do not pre-punch your stitch holes.

(13) There are at least three methods for cutting fringe and it is a

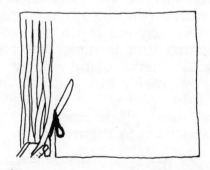

good idea to practice them all to find the one you feel most comfortable doing. (A) Using a pair of very sharp knife-edged scissors, hold the strip being fringed in your left hand. Start the cut with a two-inch snip. Hold the scissors half open and push to the sewn end of the fringe piece while pulling the narrow strip with the left hand. Do not open and close the scissors. Move from your left to the right. **(B)** Lay the piece to be fringed on a board. Place a 12-inch ruler or straight edge on the leather where you want to cut and, using a sharp razor edge, start at the top (sewn edge) and cut down to the bottom following the straight edge. In this case, move from right to left. **(C)** With a pair of very sharp scissors, use a straight cutting motion. Be sure that where you stop and restart the cut you leave a smooth edge.

In all cases, insure that the fringe is all of the same width. Fringe of 1/8 or 3/16th inch width is very attractive.

BEADING TECHNIQUES

Because of the purpose of this book, illustrations and instructions are confined to knowledge that is necessary for constructing the projects included and this should see the general craftsperson through all kinds of beadwork projects. If, however, you desire a more thorough knowledge of beads, beadwork, designs and history, we suggest that you consult **The Technique of North American Indian Beadwork** by Monte Smith.

Further, there are a limited number of beading patterns included but all of the bags and pouches in this book may be made with other patterns, taken from museums or other books, using the beading techniques illustrated herein.

Just as important is the fact that all of the bags and pouches explained in this book may be made without being beaded or they might even be adorned with quills or paint.

(1) The most important step in doing beadwork is the selection of beads. If, from the beads you have available, you select those beads that are most uniform and even, your beadwork will reflect the care that was taken. Contrarily, if you do not take the time necessary to chose uniform beads and to discard those that are misshaped and irregular, your work will show that also.

(2) Some of the contemporary beads that are readily available to most craftspersons are shown in **Figure 1**, below.

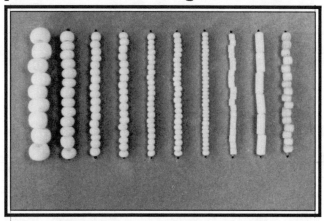

These beads are: **(a)** Pony Beads; Seed Beads **(b)** 8/°, **(c)** 10/°, **(d)** 11/°, **(e)** 12/°, **(f)** 13/°, **(g)** 14/°; **(h)** 15/° Hexigons; **(i)** Bugle Beads; and **(j)** 3-Cut Beads.

(3) As a general rule, *the larger the number, the smaller the bead.* Therefore, a size 12/° seed bead is smaller than a size 10/°

(4) Beads were first introduced into this country from Italy and what is now Czechoslovakia, but a growing source of beads is now the Orient. Czech beads are usually the most uniform but those from the Far East are getting much better. Also, in recent times France has become a good source of uniform beads.

(5) When beads are imported they come in kilos (*approximately 2.2 pounds*) and those from Czechoslovakia are on strings. These strung kilos are divided into bunches, called *hanks*, that have between 20 and 24 strings, usually 10 inches long. In that beads are imported by weight, the number of hanks per kilo varies with the size of the beads. For instance, a kilo of size 10/° beads will have about 19 hanks, whereas there are approximately 28 hanks in a kilo of size 12/° seed beads. There are more beads, regardless of whether they are on strings or in bulk, in a kilo of size 12/° beads and they usually cost more.

(6) As noted above, good beadwork starts with the selection of beads. This process starts when you purchase them and can be difficult. *First*, if you are a beginning beadworker, be sure that all of your beads are the same size: The most common size in craft stores, and the size most beginners start with, is 10/°; while many experienced beaders prefer to use size 11/° as there are more colors available in that size. *Second*, colors will often vary slightly in size; that is, a size 11/° dark blue bead may be smaller or larger than a size 11/° red bead. These problems can be overcome (see *Crowding* and *Spacing*, below), but your beading will go faster and be easier to control if the beads are all the same size when you start. *Finally*, as noted above, even in the most uniform supply of beads you are going to have ten to fifteen percent that will have to be discarded. Glass beads are still made by hand and you can expect to have some that are not uniform and even. In all cases, set these aside.

(7) Beading requires the use of needles made specifically for this purpose and come in two main classes: *Beading*, or long beading needles, and *Sharps*, or short beading needles. **Figure 2**, below, shows a number 12 needle in Beading and Sharps. As with

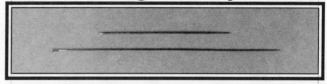

beads, *the bigger the number the smaller around the needle* and, as long as English beading needles are used, the number corresponds to the bead size. In other words, a number ten (10/°) bead calls for a number ten (10) needle. However, it is a good idea to use a needle that is smaller than the beads as many times the thread has to go through the bead a number of times. In other words, a size 11 or 12 needle with size 10/° beads will work fine.

(8) Japanese needles are numbered differently. Whereas English needles may be obtained in numbers 10, 11, 12, 13 and 15 (these relate to bead sizes), Japanese needles are usually in numbers 14 and 16 which correspond to beads, and English needles, 10 and 12, respectively. Whether English or Japanese needles are used depends on personal preference and either will work fine. Generally, English steel is very sturdy while the Japanese tends to have more flexibility or give. It's a good idea to try both and decide which works best for your style of beading.

(9) The thread that is used more than any other in beading is "nymo" or nylon and in this case *the larger the letter (or figure), the larger the thread.* Size A (or 00, 0) is the finest and it also comes in sizes B, D, and F, with F being the largest and used mostly for stringing. Of course, the size thread used depends upon the size bead and needle being used. For instance, if you are using size 13/° beads and a number 15 English beading needle you would use size A nymo; if you are using a size 10/° bead and a number 14 Japanese needle you could use a size D nymo.

The following chart will act as a guide for beginning, but this is a general outline and other combinations will work:

Beads	Needles English	Japanese	Nymo Thread
10/°	10 or 11	14	D
11/°	11 or 12	14	D
12/°	12 or 13	16	A or B
13/°	13 or 15		A

Nymo is excellent for beading in that it is extremely strong. It will, however, stretch and this can be either a benefit or liability depending upon the kind of beading being done. If the project being made will be expected to go through a great deal of bending or other stress (like a bag, pouch or belt), nymo is excellent in that it will stretch to some extent with the article it is sewn to. On the other hand, if the project will not tolerate any give at all, it might be better to use cotton or quilting thread.

(**10**) Regardless of the kind of thread used, you will want to use beeswax on it. Waxing the thread will accomplish two things: (A) It tends to make the thread stronger; and, (B) it will eliminate tangles and knots in the thread. For best results, enough wax is used to eliminate tangles but not so much that it comes off when the thread is pulled through the beads. Also, when using bugle beads, 15/° hexigon beads and Japanese cut beads, the wax will prevent the thread from being cut by the edges of these types of beads.

(**11**) It will be a matter of personal taste, but it is usually an advantage to start with a beading thread about 24 inches long. One aid in threading the needle is to make a good clean cut at an angle before waxing the thread. Then use a small amount of beeswax to make a good sharp point and run it through the eye of the needle; *needle threaders* are also available at most craft stores.

(**12**) When doing bead work it is best to have a large, well lighted area that is covered with a dish towel or desk blotter.

(**13**) The way the beads are separated will depend upon personal choice: Some beadworkers simply place all of their beads in one shallow saucer and select the beads they want to use out of it. Others will have a number of small, shallow saucers (white is probably the best color) with different colors in each one. Still other craftsmen simply make small piles of beads of different colors and select from them. Another method is to select the beads directly from the string they come on; this allows you to see which beads are uniform, to bring the beads to you when the beading thread is short and to insure that two threads will go through the hole in the beads chosen. Any of these methods, and others, will work and trying different methods will help find which works best for you.

(**14**) After you have started stringing the beads on the thread it may be that, even with the greatest of care in selection, there are times when you find that there are too many beads on a thread, or that an irregular bead has been strung. Sometimes it is easier to break the bead than take off all of the beads behind it. Breaking a bead is always a bit risky as the beads are glass and they may cut the thread. In order to minimize the risk, the bead should be broken with a pair of needlenose pliers

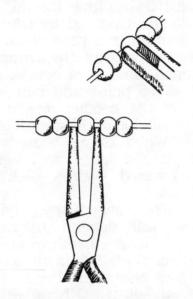

by squeezing it from the side. Never crush the bead by placing it within the jaws of the pliers and squeezing them over the thread as it is probable that the thread will be cut.

(15) While most of the projects in this book come with a possible bead-work pattern, it is probable that you will want to adopt your own patterns before too long. The best tool to use for this purpose is *Graph Paper* as it will allow you to map out the design in detail.

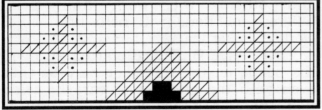

Simply find a design you like and copy it onto your graph paper. A set of colored pencils works well for this, or symbols may be used for the different colors that are going to be used. If the design will be repeated, you need only copy it once.

(16) Many beadworkers are adopting traditional techniques including the use of sinew in place of contemporary threads. These techniques are beyond the scope of this book but if you are interested in this kind of beadwork we suggest that you consult **The Technique of North American Indian Beadwork** by Monte Smith.

(17) Most beadworkers use a stitch

Traditional   **Contemporary**

that goes completely through the leather as the beads are sewn in place. It is possible, however, to use a more traditional stitch wherein the beads are sewn to the leather without going completely through it as shown above. The attractive thing about the traditional method is that the back of the beaded piece shows no threads at all. This method is a necessity when using sinew, but may also be used with nymo or waxed cotton thread.

(18) In doing the running stitch, spot stitch and return stitch, there are two methods having to do with bead spacing that will be very useful.

First, in the selection of beads, many areas will allow the use of beads that are slightly larger or smaller than the uniform ones you have selected. By looking through those beads that have been discarded, it is possible to find just the right beads for your pattern. In floral designs there are always lines that curve and many times beads that are not uniform will fit just right.

Second is a method called *Spacing* and *Crowding* of beads and this is extremely useful in backgrounds and with geometric designs. Simply put, this means either pulling beads extremely close together (crowding) or pulling them away from each other to fill more area (spacing). This is done by using the needle and thread to align the beads.

Crowding necessitates the most planning as you can only make the spaces between the beads smaller and not the beads themselves. Therefore, when it is found that the pattern will not align, it may be necessary to start pulling the beads closer together some five or six beads before the problem area. This is done by inserting the needle slightly behind the bead, going over the thread with the bead on it, taking the needle back through the leather at the point where it emerged and pulling the beads together snuggly. With pre-planning, the beads should align properly.

Spacing is making the beads fit the design by leaving *slightly* larger spaces between them and is done by using a second needle and thread slightly in front of the beads being sewn in place. It is easy to see that the use of beads that are either larger or smaller than the rest is easier. This is not always possible however, and these two techniques will be useful when needed.

(19) In doing any kind of applique beadwork, as explained in the projects that follow, it is usually easier to begin beading in the very center of the bag or pouch. This makes it much easier to "center" the beaded pattern but, even with straight lines drawn on the *wrong* side of the leather, there is often a problem with keeping the lines and beadwork straight. This happens as there is a natural tendency to pull the lines downward as the beading progresses. Often a right-handed beader will find that the far right side of the

beadwork is lower than the left side. This, of course, means that you are constantly readjusting the beadwork to keep the lines straight and match the lines drawn on the reverse of the leather.

The most reliable method to correct this tendency before it starts is to turn

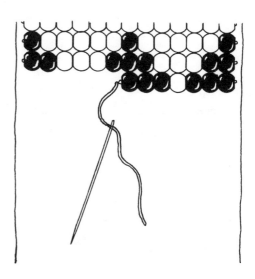

the piece around as it is being beaded, as shown above. This technique is very easy to use when beading any of the projects in this book as they are all fairly small and, therefore, easy to handle.

(20) The most important secret of doing fine craftwork and producing a "finished" product is to take your time! This means reading the project instructions through carefully and insuring that you understand how each step fits into the finished item. Make notes of anything that you want to change or personalize in the project and then, create the item with care and patience. Stitches should be evenly spaced, beads should be selected with care, fringe should all be the same width, etc., etc. Taking your time and working with patience will pay off with a finished product that will last for years.

NOTES

LEATHER POUCH

Pouches played a very important part in the life of the American Indian as almost anything of value was kept inside of one; many had very specialized purposes. In that most of the Tribes were always on the move, everything of value had to have a special place and a container to protect and maintain it.

The *Leather Pouch* described in this project is a very typical simple pouch and will introduce the basic techniques that will allow you to make other pouches and bags of almost any size and in various shapes.

Also included is a beading pattern and a list of materials needed if you choose to bead the pouch. Beading instructions, however, are not part of these instructions but they may be taken from any one of the other projects where differing techniques are described and illustrated. This beading pattern would work well with the lazy stitch, running stitch or return stitch and all of these techniques are described in this book.

MATERIALS NEEDED

1 Piece leather 4" x 18"
1 Suede thong 16" long
1 Yard imitation sinew
1 #8 Glover's or leather needle
1 Bobbin "A" thread*
1 #11 Sharps beading needles*
1 Piece beeswax*
3 Oz. 10/° white seed beads*
2 Oz. 10/° light blue seed beads*
1 Oz. 10/° dark blue seed beads*
1 Oz. 10/° yellow seed beads*

(*) Needed only if the pouch is to be beaded. These materials will be necessary to bead the enclosed beading pattern.

A   As with all projects in this book, we suggest that before beginning you read all of the instructions through carefully so that you know how each step fits into making the complete project. Do not be afraid to change or "personalize" the pouch after you understand how it is made. Then follow the instructions through step-by-step.

(1) Following the pattern enclosed, cut two pieces of leather that measure 4" x 6" (these will make the front and back of the pouch) and one piece of leather that is 3 3/4" x 6" for the fringe bottom.

(2) Keeping in mind that you will turn the pouch inside-out after sewing, place one of the larger pieces of the leather (the "front") on a flat surface

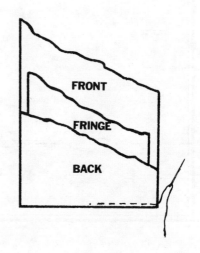

Figure 1

Figure 2

(such as a well illuminated table or work bench). Now lay the fringe piece in the center of the front piece so that there is 1/8" of the front piece showing on each side and the bottoms are even. Then lay the back piece on top of these two so that it matches the front piece exactly (**Figure 1**).

(3) Split the imitation sinew into three or four "threads" and put one of these on the leather needle making a good knot in one of the ends.

(4) Making sure that the leather pieces do not move and starting at the middle of what will be the bottom, use a running stitch (**Figure 2**) and sew the three pieces together. Stop sewing when you reach the top corner of the side. Make a knot and cut off the excess imitation sinew. Do Not sew the other end closed as this will be the top of the pouch. *NOTE:* Be sure that you do not catch the fringe piece with the needle and imitation sinew when you are sewing up the sides of the front and back.

(5) Making sure that the fringe piece has not changed position and is still in the exact center, use another thread of the imitation sinew, start again at the middle of the bottom and use the running stitch to sew the rest of the bottom and up the other side. Again, do not sew the fringe piece when going up the side. Make a good knot and cut off the excess sinew at the top corner of the pouch.

(6) Turn the pouch inside out so that the sewing is hidden and that the fringe piece hangs down.

(7) Use some sharp scissors (Be Careful) and cut the fringe into the bottom piece. Start at the bottom and cut fringe that is about 1/8" in width across the entire width of this piece. Cut these up to about 1/4" from the bottom of the pouch as shown in **Figure 3**.

(8) At even spaces about 3/4" down from the top of the pouch (as noted on the leather pattern), cut or punch eight holes (four to each side). Thread the 16" thong through these holes and knot the ends together. By pulling the ends of the thong the bag will be closed.

HINTS

(A) Any decoration such as beadwork, quillwork or painting will be easier to do on the pouch before it is sewn together. Remember, however, to leave about

Figure 3

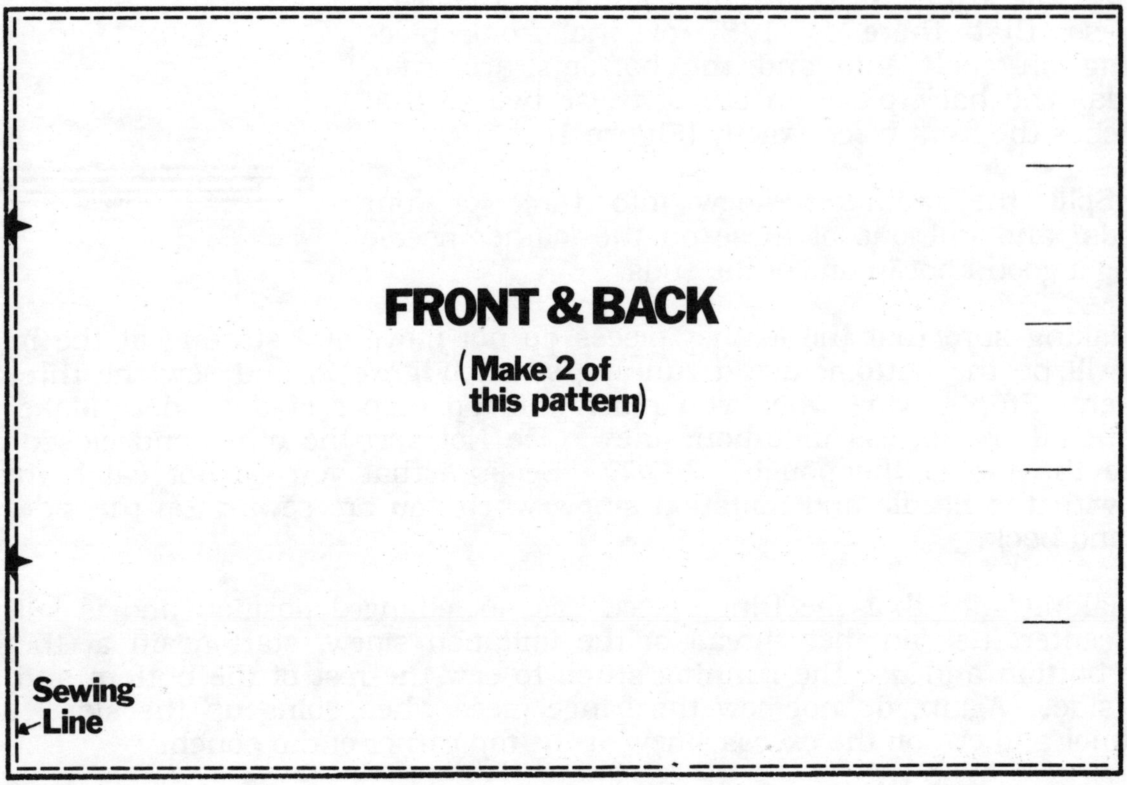

FRONT & BACK

(Make 2 of
this pattern)

Sewing
Line

FRINGE PIECE

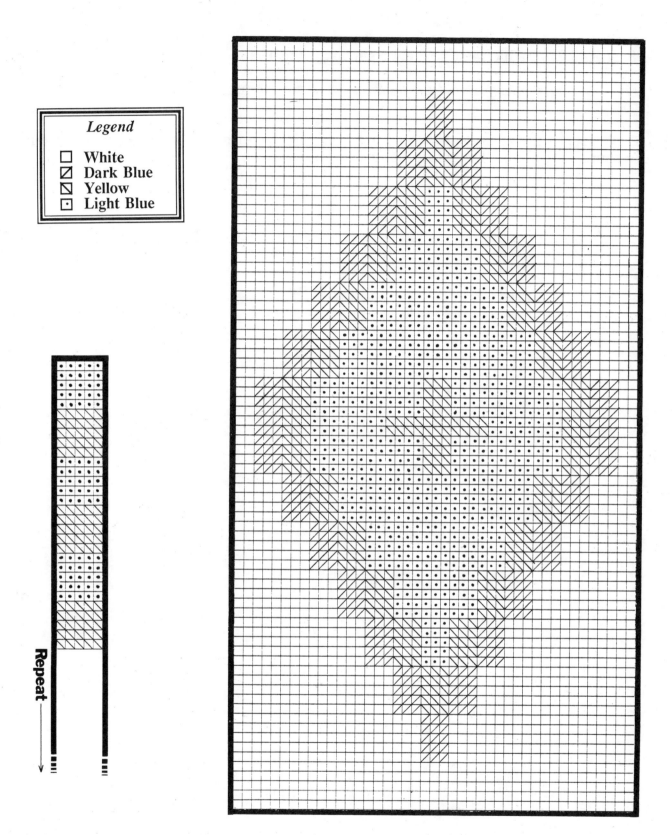

Figure 5 - Possible Beading Pattern for Leather Pouch

one-fourth (1/4") inch on each side for sewing it together.

(B) It may be easier to make the holes for the thongs before sewing the pouch together.

(C) You may want to add crow or pony beads (or even a tin cone, etc.) to the ends of the thongs for added decoration as illustrated below.

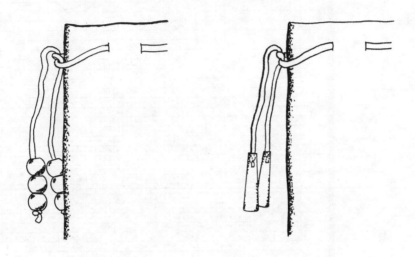

STRIKE-A-LITE POUCH

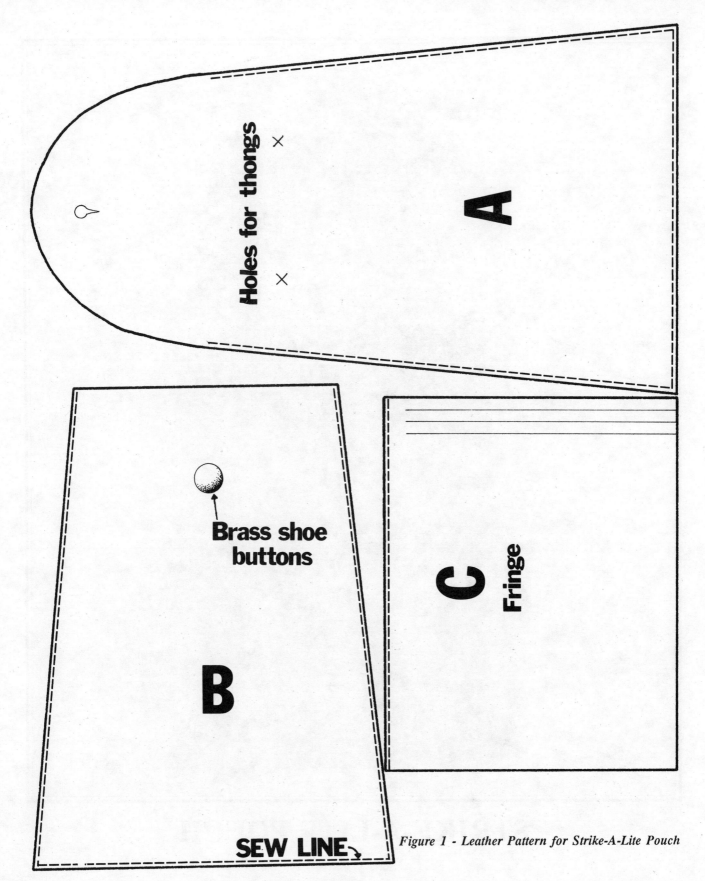

Holes for thongs

A

Brass shoe
buttons

B

C
Fringe

SEW LINE

Figure 1 - Leather Pattern for Strike-A-Lite Pouch

22

The number of specialized bags and pouches increased greatly with the coming of the fur traders and many, such as the *Strike-a-Lite Pouch*, were quickly incorporated into the daily life of the American Indian. This served as a handy place to keep flint which, because of its composition, needed a rugged, leather pouch in which to keep it safe and out of harm's way. Unless you are into instant, unplanned fires and heavy burns, we suggest that you do not keep your steel in the same container as your flint and, better yet, that you construct a separate pouch for your steel.

For a more traditional looking pouch, you will want to have the rough, or "suede" side of the leather on the outside; if you want a more "finished" looking project, use the smooth side exposed.

Be sure and read all of the instructions through before beginning. These directions include a number of bead edging techniques that may be used on this, and other, projects.

MATERIALS NEEDED

1 Piece buckskin 4 1/4" x 16"
1 Piece buckskin 1/4" x 12"
2 Crow beads
2 Medium tin cones
1 Oz. 10/° dark blue seed beads
1 Oz. 10/° white seed beads
1 Yard imitation sinew
1 #8 Glover's or leather needle
1 Bobbin "D" nymo thread
1 #10 Sharps beading needle
1 Brass shoe button

(1) Using the enclosed leather patterns, make one "Back A", one "Front B" and one piece for fringe "C". Make a small hole at each of the places marked "x" on the back "A" piece.

(2) From the imitation sinew, split it into three or four sewing threads. Put one of these on the leather needle. Then place the leather pieces as shown in **Figure 2**. To do this, place "A" on a flat surface (a well illuminated table or work bench) with the rough (suede) side toward you. Put "C" (suede side facing up) on top of "A" with the bottoms even. Then position "B" (smooth side up) on top of the other two pieces, again with the bottom aligned. Use a running stitch (**Figure 3**) and, making sure that the pieces do not move, sew all three pieces together - at the bottom only.

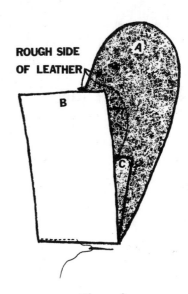

ROUGH SIDE
OF LEATHER

Figure 2

Figure 3

NOTE: If you want to have the smooth side of the pouch exposed when the project is finished, simply reverse the way the leather is laid out; the position, of course, remains the same.

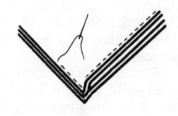

(3) As you sew the sides of "A" and "B" together (*Step 2*) making sure that you do not catch "C" with the needle and imitation sinew. Use the running stitch on all of these seams. Then turn the pouch inside-out so that the stitching is hidden and the fringe piece ("C") is hanging down. All of the pieces should be showing the suede side toward the front.

(4) Cut a slot for the shoe button in the flap as shown on the pattern for "A" and then, using another piece of split imitation sinew, sew the button on the front in the position shown on pattern "B".

(5) Into the bottom piece, cut fringe that is approximately 1/8" wide across the entire piece (**Figure 4**). On the outside fringe, string one tin cone and then one crow bead, make a small, secure knot at the very bottom of this fringe. Repeat this step on the other outside fringe. *NOTE*: If you want to personalize this project, one place to start would be to add tin cones and crow beads to more than just the outside fringe pieces.

(6) The *Edging Techniques* that are shown with this project should be self-explanatory and, while any of these are very easy to do, add a great deal to giving a "finished" appearance to this or any other bag, container or pouch. Keep in mind that edging is exposed and, therefore, takes a great deal of punishment so you should always use a double beading thread making sure that the thread is waxed well with beeswax. The necessary knots should, whenever possible, be hidden inside the bag. Plan your work so that the edging will be evenly spaced around the entire project and in this case you might want to start at the lower right-hand corner and bead completely around the bag, including the flap portion (See photo).

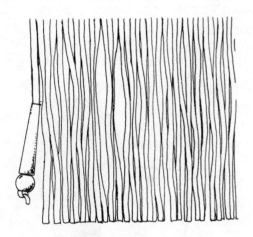

Figure 4

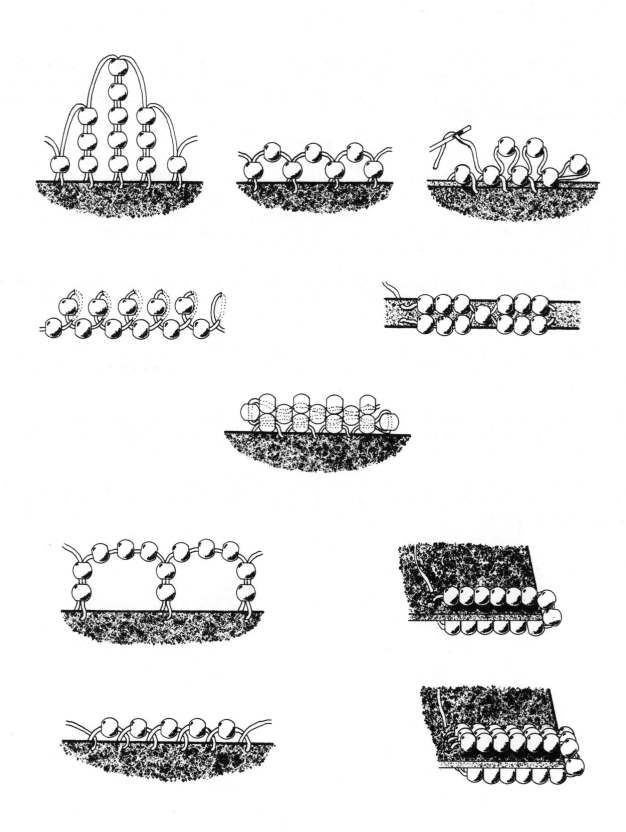

Figure 5 - Edging Techniques

25

(7) Finally, cut the 12" piece of leather into two pieces, 1/8" wide. Knot one end and thread them through the holes that were made in Step 1 (above) so that the knots are hidden inside of the pouch. These thongs are used to tie the pouch to a belt or around your neck.

HINTS

(A) It may be easier to sew on the button and make the shoe button hole before sewing the pouch together. The danger, of course, is that if you do not measure exactly and place either the hole or the button even slightly out of position it may be difficult to correct. In any event, after you make the "button hole" turn the flap down and make sure that the button is placed correctly.

(B) If you choose to add lazy stitch or applique beadwork to the front or back of the pouch, this should be done before the project is sewn together. If you do this make sure to leave room at the sides for the sewing.

(C) Make sure that the fringe piece ("C") does not get sewn into your stitching as you attach the sides of "A" and "B" together and that you always use a good, neat, evenly spaced stitch.

(D) Do not hesitate to split the imitation sinew into three or four sewing threads as it will still be very strong. This will also make getting the imitation sinew on the needle and doing the actual sewing much easier.

(E) Step 5 (Page 24) may be done without the crow beads. In this case you simply string a tin cone on the fringe, make a secure knot and then slide the tin cone down over the knot.

KNIFE SHEATH

27

The knife sheath was, of course, one of the most important containers used by the American Indian and the fur traders. Most, as with the one described in this project, were not placed on a belt but were carried inside the pants or breechclout next to the body with the hilt showing for easy access. If you are making this knife sheath for a particular knife, the measurements and pattern should be changed to reflect your needs.

This is one of the few projects wherein any beading or quilling that is desired should be done after the *Knife Sheath* has been completely sewn together. Included is a beading pattern and a list of needed materials, but specific beading instructions are not provided. These, however, may be adopted from any of the other projects in this book and the enclosed beading pattern was chosen as it goes well with either the running, return or lazy stitch; the pattern may, of course, be repeated if you want to bead the entire project. One of the nice things about beading a project of this kind is that you have a rawhide backing that will "guide" the needle and make the work much easier.

As with all craft projects, we strongly suggest that you read all of the instructions through carefully before beginning construction so that you understand how each step fits into making the finished sheath. Should you want to "personalize" the project, make notes of any desired changes as you go through the directions and then make them part of the final instructions. Further, you will find that many of the techniques used in this project will be useful in making a number of American Indian craft items.

MATERIALS NEEDED

 1 Piece rawhide 8" x 5"
 1 Piece buckskin 8 1/2" x 5 1/2"
18 Inches beading wire^
24 Inches imitation sinew
 1 #8 Glover's or leather needle
 1 Bobbin "A" thread*
 1 #11 Sharps beading needle*
 1 Piece beeswax*
 1 Oz. 10/° blue seed beads*
 1 Oz. 10/° white seed beads*
 1 Oz. 10/° red seed beads*
 3 Oz. 10/° green seed beads*

(^) You may substitute with copper or any other kind of wire that is sturdy and malleable.

(*) These materials are only needed if the sheath is to be beaded using the enclosed beading pattern.

(1) From the rawhide, cut out the inner sheath following the pattern that is provided. If you desire to make a sheath to fit a smaller knife, use the knife for a pattern but be sure and leave room for stitching. Then, with an awl or other pointed instrument (Be Careful), make holes as shown in the pattern.

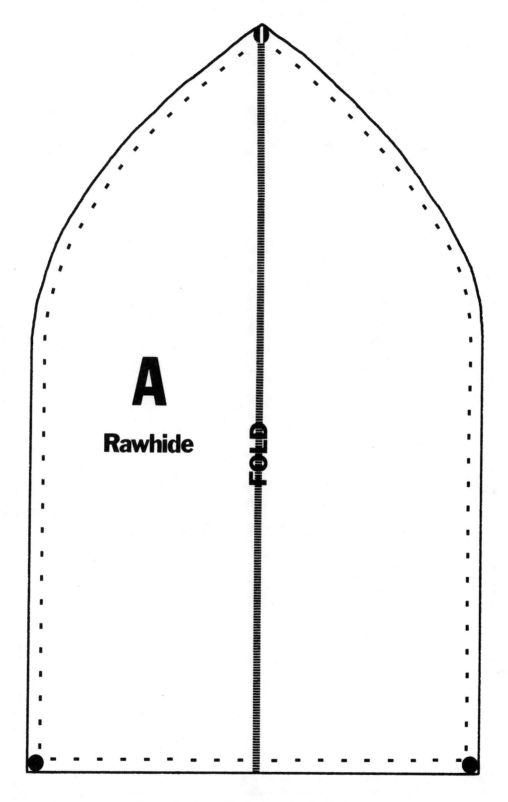

Figure 1 - Rawhide Pattern for Knife Sheath

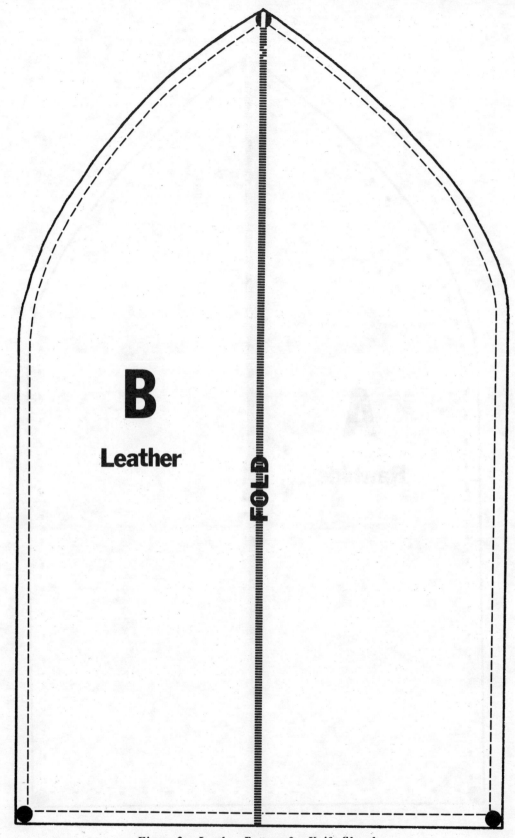

B

Leather

FOLD

Figure 2 - Leather Pattern for Knife Sheath

30

(2) Bend the rawhide piece in half at the fold line. Do Not press the rawhide flat as it should form a curve(!) and if you "fold" the pieces together they will stay that way. With the beading wire, lace the sides together using the holes that were made in *Step 1* (**Figure 3**). Do not lace the top as these holes will be used later. If you want to add "dangles" or anything to the bottom of the sheath, do that as you lace the rawhide.

(3) Following the pattern, cut out the leather piece or "outside sheath." This will only be your initial cutting and the leather will have to be adjusted as noted below.

Figure 3

(4) The leather must fit snugly around the rawhide. So, fold the leather around the rawhide and, matching the large dots on the pattern and making sure all corners and edges are even, use a small piece of imitation sinew on a needle and "tack" the leather piece in place around the rawhide. (*NOTE*: A "tack" is simply a small, single stitch to hold everything in place and these may be removed when the final stitching is done. You usually tack at the top, in the middle and at the bottom.) Keep in mind that the leather will stretch a certain amount and trim the sides so that the leather extends just beyond the rawhide and is even at the top. Re-tack when necessary.

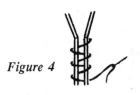

Figure 4

(5) With a whip stitch (**Figure 4**), use a thread of the imitation sinew to attach the leather to the rawhide at the top of the sheath following the holes in the rawhide as a guide (**Figure 5**).

(6) Starting at the top corner of the leather, stitch the side seams together with imitation sinew using an inside-out stitch (**Figure 6**). This will create a tight fit over the rawhide. Double stitch all of the corners for extra strength.

(7) It is possible to add a belt loop to the sheath and if you choose to do so use some leather and attach it at the corner of the leather and rawhide making sure that the loop is secure.

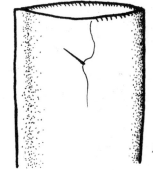

Figure 5

HINTS

(A) Take your time as you construct the sheath and think about how everything goes together. If you want to make any changes, make notes and plot how to make them part of the finished product.

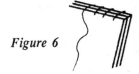

Figure 6

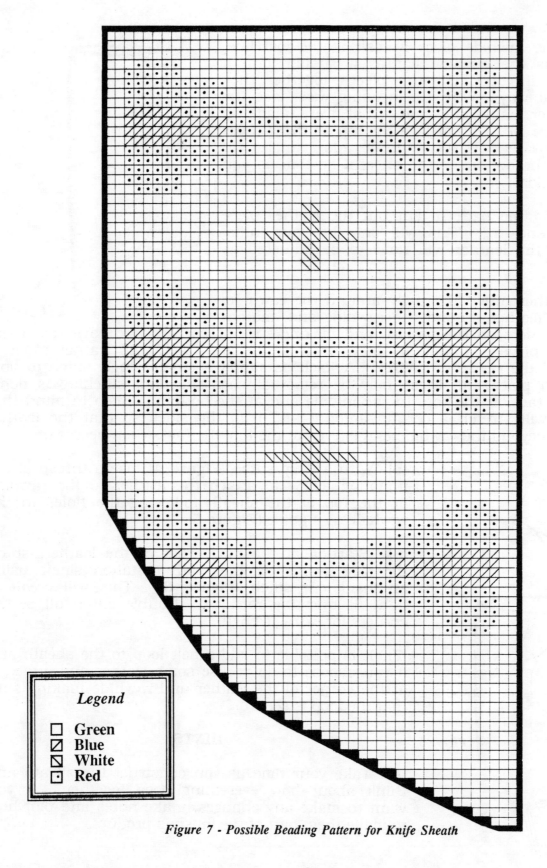

Figure 7 - Possible Beading Pattern for Knife Sheath

(B) The imitation sinew may be used full strength but we suggest that it be split into three or four sewing threads. This will make it easier to use and it will still be very strong.

(C) The leather may be beaded before it is sewn together, but it takes some planning. Beading on the leather tends to contract the leather slightly and if the beading is to be done first, allow extra leather for possible adjustment - about 1/2" will do. Be sure that you leave enough room at the top and side edges to sew the leather. You will want to start at the center and work toward each side following the outline of the sheath precisely! After it has been beaded you may sew the leather to the rawhide, fill in any small gaps which may appear in the beadwork, then use an edging technique (shown in this book) to cover the seams. Or, you can use a return stitch and fill in the spaces between beads at the seams and at the top.

(D) In choosing which side of the leather is to be exposed, keep in mind that it will be easier to bead with the smooth side out but that the knife sheath will look more "traditional" or "primitive" if the suede side is showing.

NOTES

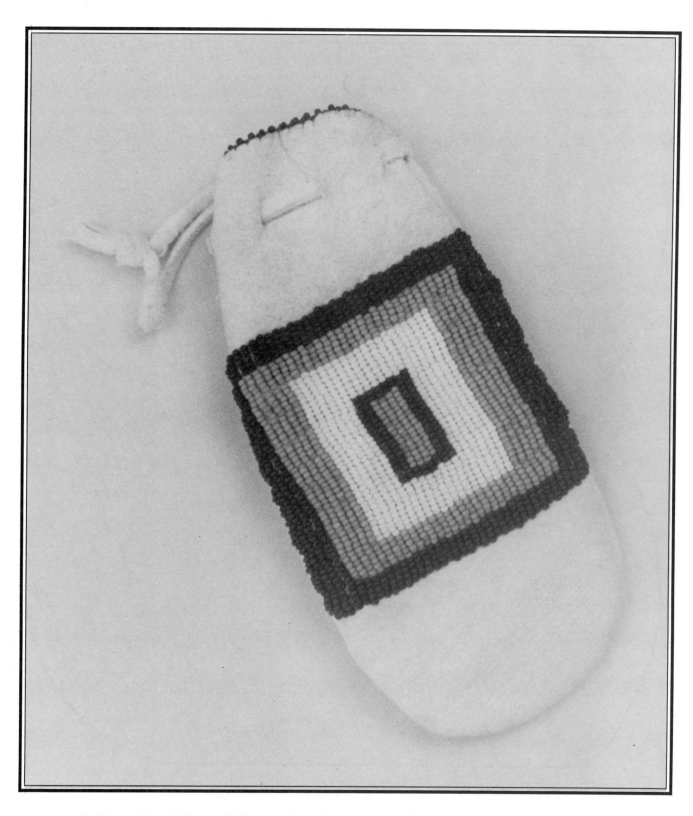

BEADED SIOUX POUCH (Lazy Stitch)

35

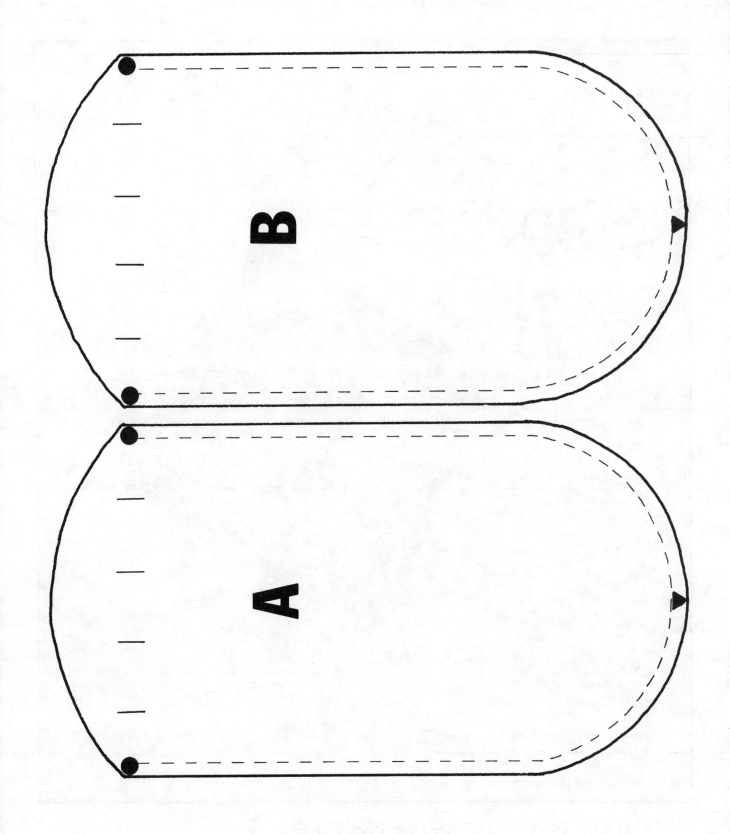

Figure 1 - Leather Pattern for Beaded Sioux Pouch

A fine little round-top pouch with beading instructions for the *Lazy Stitch* technique.   As with all of the projects in this book, the pouch may be made without beading.

MATERIALS NEEDED

1   Split leather piece - 8" x 7 3/4"
1   Suede thong - 12" long
2   Feet imitation sinew
1   #8 Glover's or leather needle
1   Bobbin "A" thread
1   #11 beading needle
1   Piece beeswax
1   Oz 10/° white seed beads
1   Oz 10/° light blue seed beads
2   Oz 10/° dark blue seed beads

(1)   Following the pattern with this project, cut out two pieces of leather.   Put the back piece aside as only the front piece ("A") will be beaded.

(2)   The lazy stitch has become one of the most popular beading techniques because of the "flow" of the appearance and the speed with which it is possible to cover large areas. It is easier to explain the stitch than to do it, so take your time and do not be afraid to take out the first two or three rows and start again after the technique is mastered.

(3)   Begin by cutting about 24" of thread from the bobbin, put it on the beading needle and pull the thread across the beeswax to wax it. Knot one end so that you can pull the thread through the needle as you bead and only one thread goes through each bead. Then you want to "center" the pattern on the leather.

(4)   The space that will be covered in beading will depend upon the size and shape of the beads used and the easiest way to make sure the pattern is in the middle of the leather is to start at the center. So find the exact middle of the front piece and bring the needle from the back through the leather at that point. The needle and thread should be coming out of the smooth side in the center of the leather.

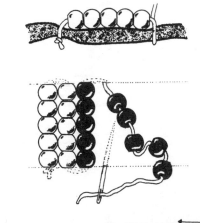

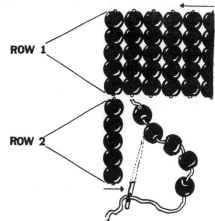

ROW 1

ROW 2

Figure 2

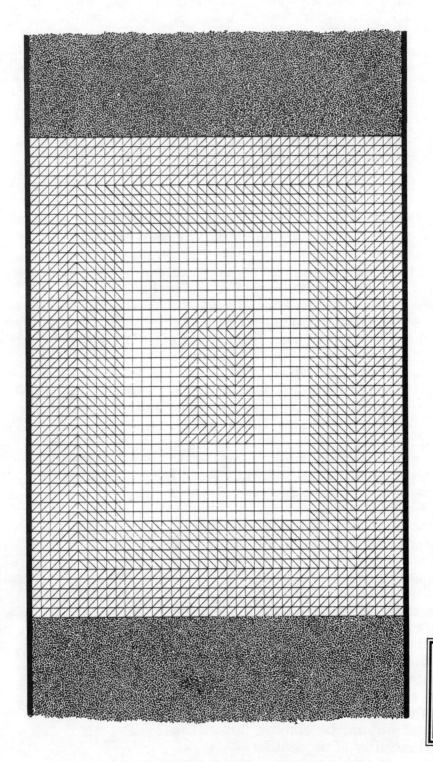

Figure 3 - Possible Beading Pattern for Beaded Sioux Pouch

38

(5) Lazy stitch may be done with five to seven beads, but in this project you will use five beads at a time. String five light blue beads on the thread, push the beads close together and, even with the last bead (**Figure 2**), take the needle down through the leather. Pull snug. Then bring the needle up through the leather 1/2 bead width to the right and even with the top bead. This does take some practice and some horizontal lines drawn with a pencil on the back of the leather may be helpful. Place five light blue beads on the thread and go back down through the leather even with the bottom bead of the last row. Then back up through the leather, string five dark blue beads on the thread, etc. following the pattern with this project and moving to the right. *NOTE:* The pattern will not cover all of the leather and if you want a fully beaded pouch, continue beading after you reach the end of the beading pattern with dark blue beads but do not go any closer than 1/4" from the edge. When the row is finished to the right, either knot and start from the center again or weave the thread through the stitching on the back until you reach the middle (where you started), and bead from the center to the left.

(6) The next row down starts directly under the last bead on the left and is beaded from left to right. One of the secrets of lazy stitch is to keep the rows in a straight line, so follow this same technique on the row while following the pattern; the next row down will go from right to left and so forth. When the bottom half of the beading is complete, knot securely on the back, turn the leather around and bead the top half. This time you can start at either side.

(7) There is a pattern included for edging around the top of the pouch. This may be done now or, if you wait until the project is sewn together, you may edge the front and back at the same time.

(8) Keep in mind that the Pouch will be turned inside-out after sewing. Place "Pouch A" on top of "Pouch Back B" matching the dots and circles and the outside seams. With the imitation sinew, start in the middle of the bottom and, making sure the pieces remain in place, sew along the bottom and up the right side to the top corner (**Figure 4**). Make a good knot and cut off the excess thread. Now go back to the middle of the bottom and sew from there up the left side.

(9) Now turn the pouch inside-out and carefully work the corners out so that the bag lays flat.

(10) Cut the drawstring slits at the top of the bag as shown on the pattern. Then, as shown in **Figure 5**, thread the suede thong through the holes.

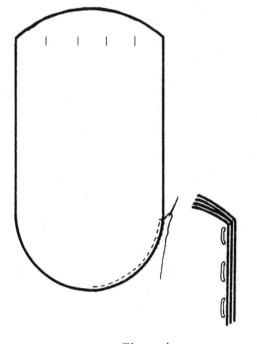

Figure 4

39

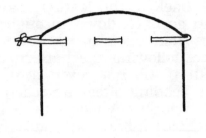

Figure 5

HINTS

(A) Take your time as you put the project together.   If you want to make changes, plot how to make them part of the finished item.

(B)   The imitation sinew may be used full strength, but it will be easier to use on the needle if it is split into three or four strong "threads."

(C)   The Pouch may be made without decoration but be sure you do any beading that is desired before it is sewn together.

(D)   The reason you use an uneven number of beads in the Lazy Stitch (*Step 5*) is to allow you to achieve points in geometric designs

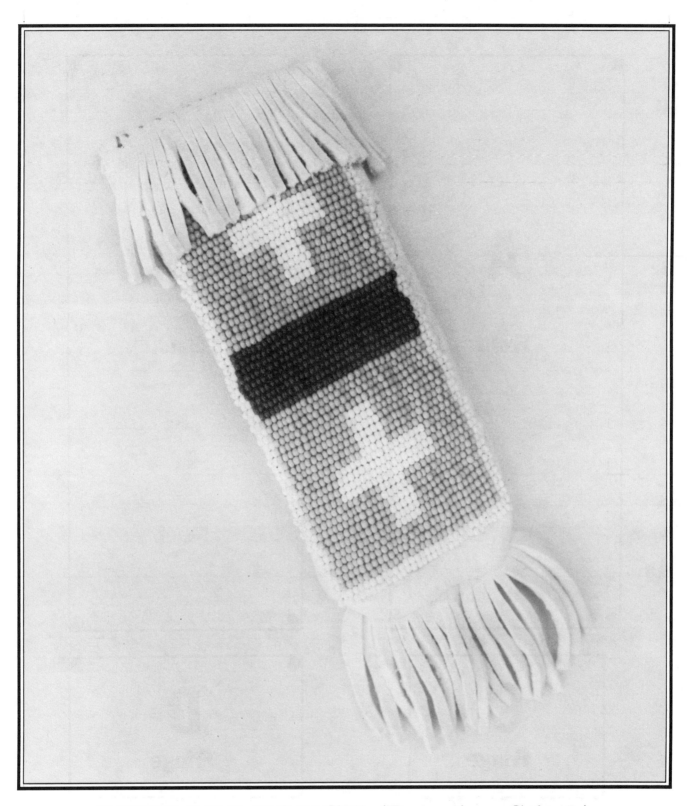

SCISSORS POUCH (Running Stitch)

41

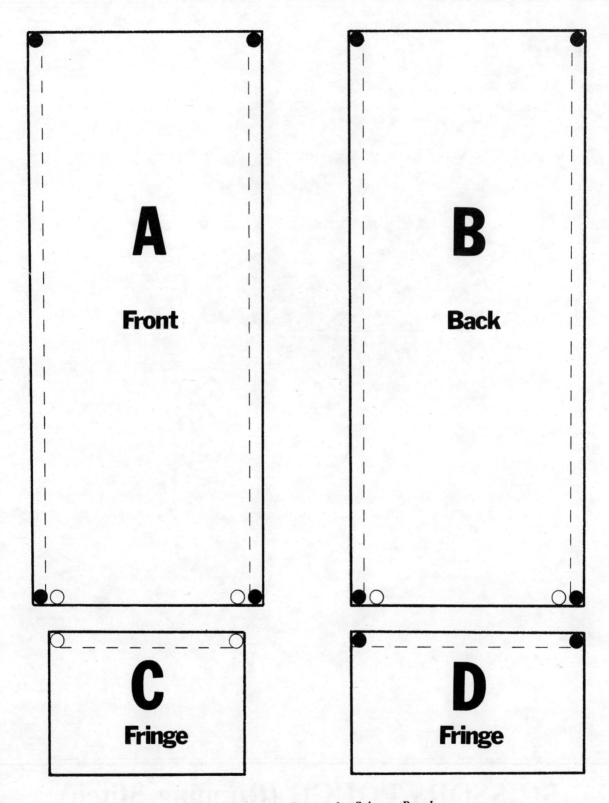

Figure 1 - Leather Pattern for Scissors Pouch

This is a very nice little bag that would be called a *Scissors Pouch* in the Reservation Period of the American Indian or a "Possibles Pouch" by the mountain men. This project includes complete instructions for an applique beading technique called the *Running Stitch* that may be used with all kinds of Indian craftwork.

MATERIALS NEEDED

1 Buckskin piece 5" x 7 1/2"
2 Feet imitation sinew
1 #8 Glover's or leather needle
1 Bobbin "A" thread
2 #12 Beading needles
1 Piece beeswax
1 Oz 11/° dark blue seed beads
2 Oz 11/° white seed beads
3 Oz 11/° light blue seed beads

(1) Following the leather pattern, cut out the four (4) pieces of leather. Make sure that you plan your cutting so that you get all of the pieces out of the minimum amount of leather. Put three (3) of the leather pieces to the side as only the Pouch Front "A" will be beaded.

(2) The "running stitch" is a very good way to do applique (or overlay) beading and it is done with two needles. To start, cut about 24" of thread from the bobbin and put on a needle. Pull the thread through so that the ends are even and the needle is in the middle and knot the ends together. Pull this thread (the "beading thread") across the beeswax to wax it. Cut another 24" thread, put it on a needle and pull about 8" of the thread through the needle. Make a knot in the end of the long (16") end of this thread and pull it (the "spotting thread") across the beeswax. You will now have one double beading thread that will go through the beads and a single-strand spotting thread that will be used to hold the beads in position. The needle may be moved up on the spotting thread as the beading progresses as only one end has been tied in a knot.

(3) As in all beading, the space that will be covered with your beading will depend upon the size and shape of the beads that you use, and the easiest way to make sure the pattern is in the middle of the leather is to start at the center. So find the exact middle of the front ("A") piece and bring the needle with the beading thread from the back through the leather at that point. The needle and thread should be coming out of the smooth side in the center of the leather. As the running stitch is a series of horizontal rows, it may be helpful to draw a straight line from edge to edge of the leather that passes

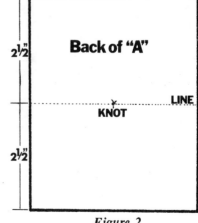

Figure 2

43

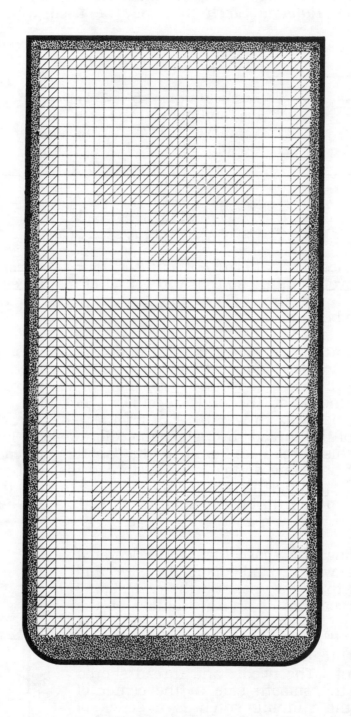

Figure 3 - Possible Beading Pattern for Scissors Pouch

through the center point (where the knot is) and is even with the top and bottom of the piece (**Figure 2**). As you work your way down the piece with rows of beads, it might help further to make more light pencil lines (on the reverse of the leather piece, of course) to make sure that your beaded rows are straight and orderly.

(**4**) Now find the exact center of the beading pattern that comes with this project and count the number of beads (including the center one) from there to the right side of the pattern. If you use the enclosed beading pattern, there are 13 blue beads and 2 white beads. String those beads on the beading thread, pull them snug (but not tight) against each other and, even with the outside of the last bead, take the needle down through the leather so that the needle goes through the line drawn on the back. Then, bring the needle with the spotting thread through the leather from the back at a point between the third and fourth beads; the needle should come through the line that was drawn. Take the spotting thread over the beading thread and back through the same hole used in coming up (**Figure 4**). Bring the spotting thread back up through the leather three or four beads further along, go over the beading thread and back down through the leather and so forth along this row so that it has all been tacked down.

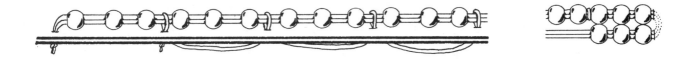

Figures 4 and 5

(**5**) For the next row, the beading thread is brought back up through the leather directly below the end of the first row (**Figure 5**); this row is, of course, exactly the width of one bead below the first row. When this point is known, you may want to draw another line on the back of the leather parallel to the others that have been drawn. Now string 2 white beads, 25 blue beads and 2 white beads on the beading thread, pull them snug and take the needle down through the leather to the far left side. Then use the spotting thread to tack this row into place.

Some important "secrets" in using this technique are: (**A**) Select and use beads that are even and the same size; throw away any and all irregular beads. (**B**) The spotting thread is used to keep the beads in neat rows both across the beadwork and up and down. This becomes very important when you get to the pattern (the fifth row) and you should always use the spotting thread between the beads when you change colors! This will help keep the pattern neat and attractive. (**C**) The stitch may be used by stringing ten or twelve beads on the beading thread (instead of a full row), tacking them down, stringing more beads, tacking, etc. (**D**) It is not necessary to draw the line on the back for every row, but one every inch or so will often be helpful after the first couple of rows.

(6) Continue with the technique in *Step 5* until the bottom half of the pouch is complete. Then turn the leather around, start again in the middle and bead the top half of the bag. When the beading has been completed and you are ready to stitch the pouch together, go to the next step. If you decide to bead both sides of the pouch or even the top fringe piece, these should be done at this stage and before the pouch is sewn together.

(7) Before sewing, it is important to note that the pouch will be turned inside out after you have put it together. So, place "Fringe C" on top of "Pouch Back B" matching the dots and circles and the outside seams. Then place "Pouch Front A" on top of these two pieces so the beading is on the inside and the bottoms of all three pieces are even (**Figure 6**). Now pull the top of "C" in and out of the way, and stitch up the right side sewing "B" and "A" together up to the top outside corner. Make a good knot and cut off the excess thread.

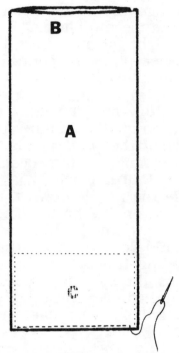

Figure 6

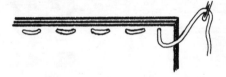

Figure 7

(8) Start again at the lower left-hand corner and, keeping "C" out of the stitch, sew the left sides of "A" and "B" together. Make sure that "C" (the fringe piece) does not get sewn with "A" and "B". Then sew "C" into place. All of the sewing in this project may be done with a simple running stitch (**Figure 7**).

Figure 8

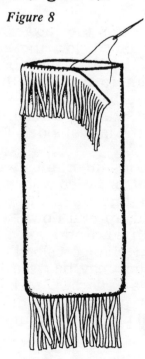

(9) Turn the pouch inside-out so that the fringe piece hangs down. As shown in **Figure 8**, use a whip stitch and sew "Fringe D" to the top of "Pouch A" starting at the left side and continuing around to the right one.

(10) Finally, cut the fringe in "C" and "D" by making cuts that are about 1/8" in width.

HINTS

(A) Take your time as you put the project together. If you want to make any changes, plot how to make them part of the finished item before beginning construction.

(B) The imitation sinew may be used full strength, but it will be helpful if you split it into three or four "threads" before sewing. It will be easier to get on the needle, easier to sew and will still be strong enough to insure a good strong stitch.

(C) "Tie strings" may be added to the back of the pouch in order to keep items secure inside of it or to keep it tied to your belt or even around your neck.

(D) The project may be made without decoration but any beading that is to be done should be completed before sewing the pouch together.

(E) When the pouch is beaded it will be easier if the smooth side of the leather is on the outside; making it so that the rough or suede side is shown will give the pouch a more "primitive" look.

(F) Almost any stitch may be used, but you will find the running stitch to be relatively easy and very fast. Be sure and make nice, evenly-spaced stitches for a more attractive finished product.

NOTES

BEADED CROW POUCH (Crow Stitch)

53

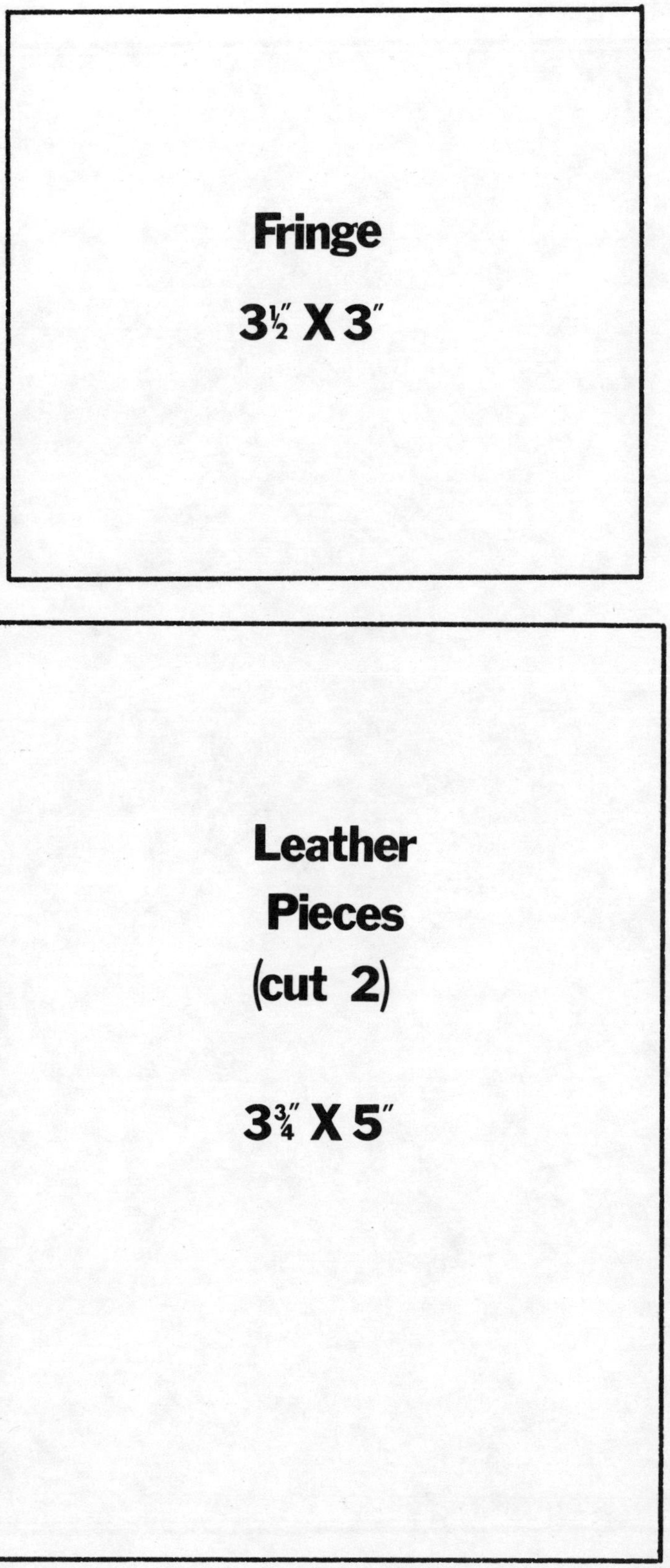

Fringe

3½" X 3"

Leather
Pieces
(cut 2)

3¾" X 5"

Figure 1 - Leather Pattern for Crow Pouch

54

A small, attractive pouch with an open top and instructions for beading it with the beautiful *Crow Stitch*. This beading technique is similar to the running stitch shown with other projects in this book but features intersecting rows of beads that give it a distinct appearance. This is an enjoyable project that makes into a most appealing pouch.

MATERIALS NEEDED

1	Buckskin piece - 3 3/4" x 13"
2	Feet imitation sinew
1	#8 Glover's or leather needle
1	Piece beeswax
1	Bobbin "A" thread
2	#12 sharps beading needles
3	Oz 11/° light blue seed beads
2	Oz 11/° dark blue seed beads
2	Oz 11/° light green seed beads
1	Oz 11/° dark green seed beads
1	Oz 11/° red seed beads
2	Oz 11/° yellow seed beads
2	Oz 11/° white seeds beads

(1) Following the enclosed leather pattern, cut two pieces that measure 3 3/4" x 5" (these will make the front and back) and one leather piece that is 3 1/2" x 3" (for the fringed bottom and may be longer if desired).

(2) Set the fringe piece to one side for later use as either the front or back (or both) may now be beaded. There are two typical Crow designs included with this project and you should decide which one to use. Now, with a pencil, trace the pattern on the back of the piece to be beaded and this will serve as a guide. Keep in mind that the pouch will be sewn together and that the design should not be any closer than 1/4" from the outside of the leather.

(3) **Figure 2** and **Figure 3** show the "modified lazy" or Crow Stitch. As noted before, these instructions are the minimum needed to produce nice beadwork and if you are interested in complete details and many secrets of beading it is suggested that you obtain a copy of **The Techniques of North American Indian Beadwork** by Monte Smith.

Figure 2

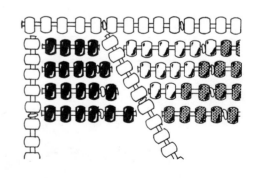

Figure 3

55

(4) The crow stitch is done with two (2) needles: Cut a comfortable amount of beading thread (about 24") off of the bobbin, thread it through one needle and knot one end only. As you bead, the thread can be pulled up through the needle so that only a single strand of thread goes through each bead. Then wax the thread by pulling it across the beeswax. Now do this same thing with another thread and needle.

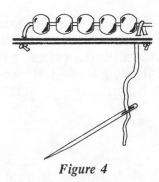

Figure 4

(5) One of the unique techniques of Crow-style beading is the use of "borders" and the first step is to bead these in place - the borders on the enclosed patterns are shown with white beads. One needle is taken through the back of the leather at the top of the border design and about five white beads are strung on it. The other needle is brought through the leather from the back, even with the last (fifth) bead and goes over the thread with the beads on it and back through the leather holding the beads in place (**Figure 4**). Then about five more beads are put on the beading thread, the second needle is brought back through the leather at that point and used to tack the beading down as before and so forth along the border row. At the end of a row, the needle with the beading thread is taken down through the leather and brought back up at the beginning of the new border row until all borders have been beaded in place.

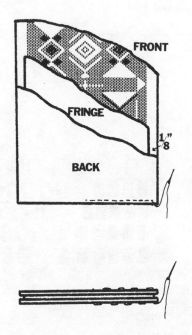

Figure 5

(6) The body of the beading is done with the same technique except that it is done in rows across the pouch. Start at one side, inside the side border and below the top border, and work across the top row as shown in **Figure 3**. Be careful to change colors at the proper places and to work within the borders. Be sure and knot carefully any place where you end a beading thread and have to start another.

(7) When the beading is finished, the pieces are ready for sewing. Keeping in mind that the pouch will be turned inside-out after sewing, place the front leather piece on a table with the beads toward you. Now lay the fringed piece on the center bottom of the front piece so that there is 1/8" showing on both sides. Then lay the back piece on top of these two so that it matches the front piece exactly (**Figure 5a**). *NOTE*: If you choose to bead the back of the pouch also, it should be done before this step and when you place it on top of the other two pieces, make sure that the beading is down (facing away from you).

(8) Split the imitation sinew into three or four threads and put one of these on the leather needle and make a knot in one end.

(9) Making sure that the leather pieces do not move and starting at the middle of what will be the bottom, use a simple running stitch (**Figure 5b**) and sew the three pieces together. Stop sewing when you reach the top of the side; make a knot and cut off the excess thread. Do Not sew the top end closed. *NOTE:* Be sure that you do not catch the fringe piece with the needle and imitation sinew as you sew up the sides of the front and back! Now, go back to the middle of the bottom and sew up the other side.

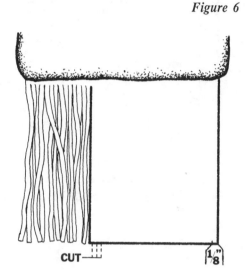

Figure 6

(10) Carefully turn the pouch inside-out so that the fringe piece is now on the outside (at the bottom) and the beadwork is exposed. You may have to work at the corners but they will lay flat with a bit of effort.

(11) Use some sharp scissors (Be careful) and cut the fringe into the bottom piece. Start at the bottom of the piece and cut fringe that is about 1/8" wide. Cut these up to about 1/4" from the bottom of the pouch as illustrated in **Figure 6**.

HINTS

(A) If you want to quill this or any other project, you may want to consult **The Techniques of Porcupine Quill Decoration Among the Indians of North America** by William C. Orchard. For further information about this beading technique, see **Crow Indian Beadwork** by Wildschut and Ewers.

(B) As with any of the new beading techniques introduced in these pages, try the *Crow Stitch* on another project. This is a most beautiful type of beadwork.

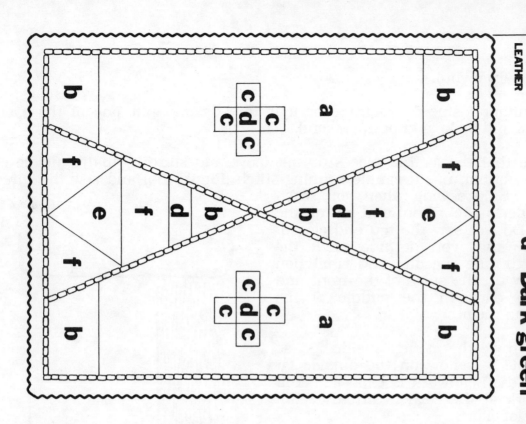

Color code

a	Powder blue	**e = Red or**
b	Dark blue	**cheyenne pink**
c	Light green	**f = Yellow**
d	Dark green	**○ = White**

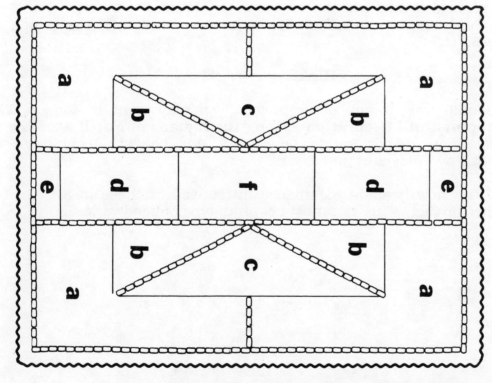

Figure 7 - Possible Beading Patterns for Crow Pouch

58

FRINGED POUCH (Rosette)

59

The instructions below produce a nice, little pouch with fringe on both sides and include complete illustrated directions for making a beaded rosette. *Rosettes* are, of course, used extensively in the craft work of the American Indian and with the basic techniques explained herein, you can make them of almost any size.

MATERIALS NEEDED

1 Buckskin piece 4" x 8"
1 Buckskin piece 9" x 5"
2 Feet imitation sinew
1 #8 Glover's or leather needle
1 Bobbin "A" thread
2 #11 sharps beading needle
1 Piece beeswax
1 Oz. 11/° blue seed beads
1 Oz. 11/° white seed beads

(1) Following the pattern, cut out the four (4) pieces of leather. Make sure that you pre-plan your cutting so that you can get the total project out of the least amount of leather. Then set all of the pieces aside except for "B" (Pouch Front) as this is the piece that will be beaded.

(2) Beading the rosette is done with a technique called "spot stitching" and is accomplished with two (2) needles. Cut about a 24" thread from the bobbin, put it on a needle, pull the thread through so that the ends are even and the needle is in the middle, and knot the ends together. Pull this thread (called the "beading thread") across the beeswax to wax it. Cut another 24" thread, put it on another needle and pull about 8" of the thread through the needle. Make a knot in the end of the long (16") end of the thread and pull this thread (called the "spotting thread") across the beeswax. You will now have one double beading thread that will go through the beads and a single strand spotting thread. The needle will be moved up the thread as the beading progresses.

(3) Find the center of leather piece "B" and bring the needle and beading thread through the leather at that point so that it comes out of the smooth side (the knot will be on the rough or suede side) in the middle of the pouch front. String one bead (if you choose to use the enclosed beading pattern, this will be a white bead) on the beading thread and go back through the leather as

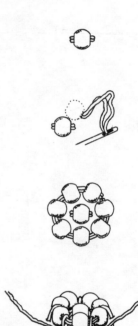

Figure 1

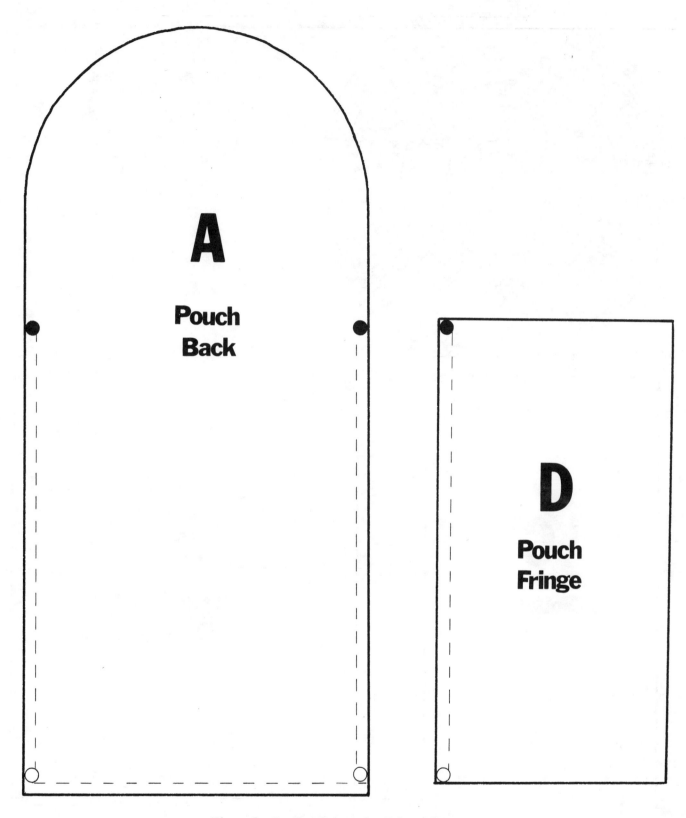

Figure 2 - Leather Pattern for Fringed Pouch

61

Figure 3 - Leather & Beading Pattern for Fringed Pouch

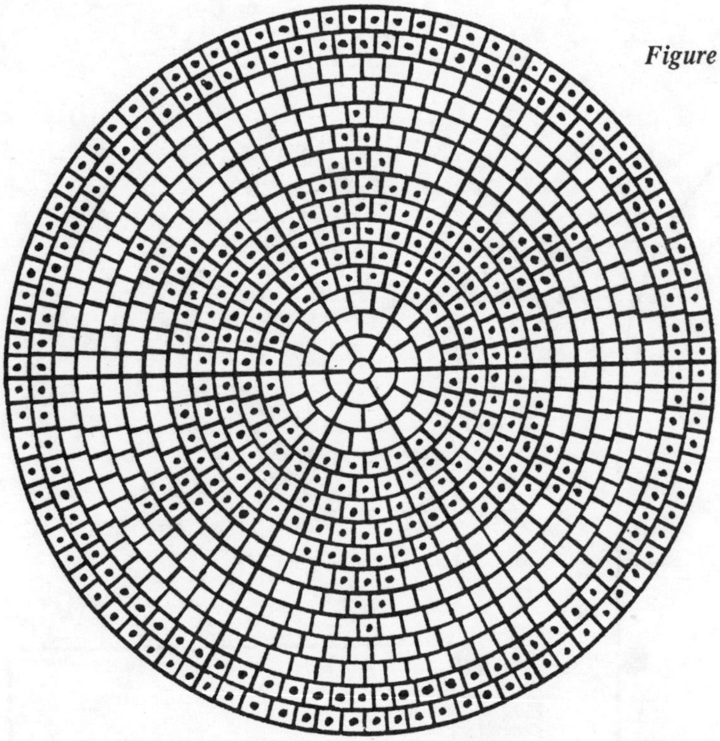

Legend

☐ White
☑ Blue

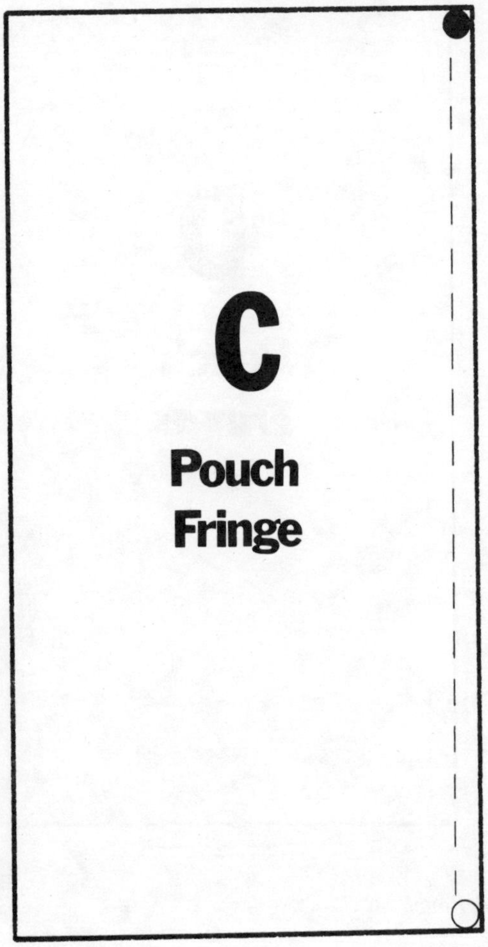

C
Pouch
Fringe

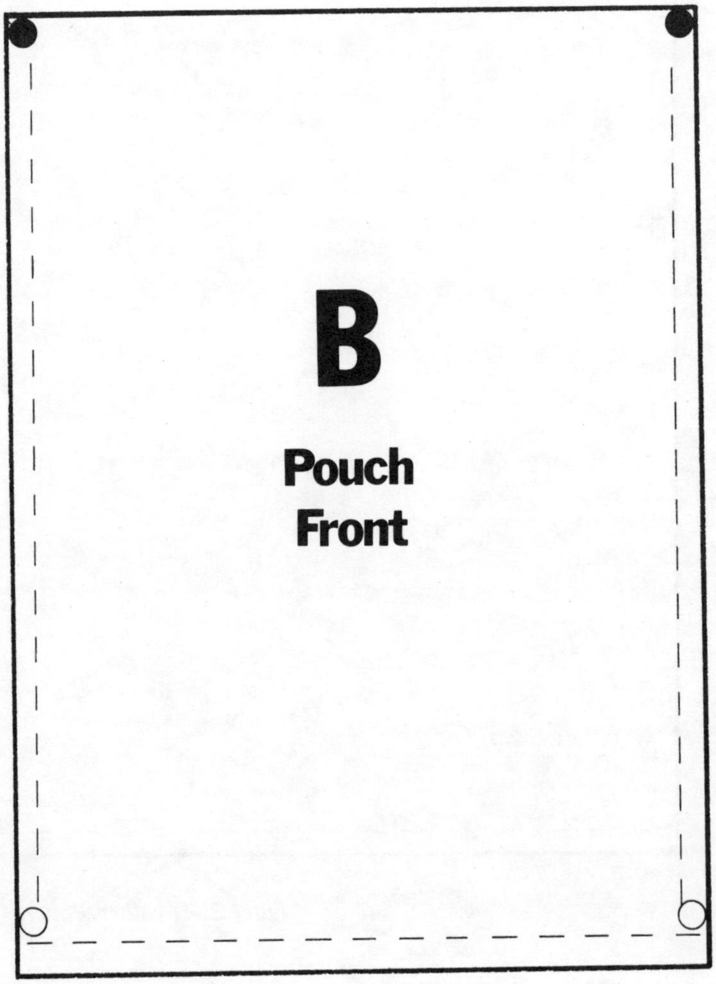

B
Pouch
Front

shown in **Figure 1**. Then bring the beading thread back through the leather so that it comes out slightly more than 1/2 bead width from the center bead, string enough beads to go around the center bead and take the needle with the beading thread back through the leather. The number of beads in this row will depend upon the size of the beads being used (usually, however, six to eight beads) and this is the hardest row to get into place.

(**4**) After the beads are placed so that they almost touch the center bead, bring the needle with the spotting thread through the leather from the back so that it emerges next to the thread between two of the beads. Take it over the beading thread and go back through the leather. Next bring the spotting thread back up through the leather so that it comes out next to the thread between the next two beads, then go over the beading thread and back through the leather. For this row it is best to spot between each bead, but as you get farther from the center the spotting can be between every second bead and then every third.

(**5**) As each row is beaded into place, keep the leather flat and allow a tiny space between the rows. If the beads touch, it will create a curved surface on the leather. The next row can be sewn in place with the same technique, but be careful to fit them in (using the spotting thread) so that the design is made as desired. The use of beads that are either slightly larger or smaller than the others will be useful in spots.

(**6**) When the rosette is completed it should lie perfectly flat (See "*Hints A*"). If it does not, it usually means that the thread has been pulled too tightly and that, of course, forces the beads together. As with all beadwork, it requires practice and patience to produce award-winning work. Do not give up as excellent beadwork may be produced in a surprisingly short period of time.

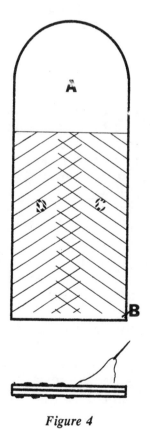

Figure 4

(**7**) You may now construct the pouch: Keeping in mind that the pouch will be turned inside out after sewing, place "Fringe C" on top of "Pouch Back A" matching the dots and circles and the outside seams. The bottom of the fringe piece will be about 1/8" from the bottom of the pouch back. Then place "Pouch Front B" (with the beaded rosette away from you or facing down) on top of these two pieces matching the bottom of "A" and the sides of "A" and "C". With these three pieces on top of each other, and making sure they do not move, use some of the imitation sinew and sew the right seam together from the bottom to the top of piece "B". Make a good knot and cut off the excess thread.

(8) As shown in **Figure 4**, insert "Fringe D" between "A" and "B", matching the dots and circles, and on the left seam stitch the pieces together keeping the edges even.

(9) Now sew the bottom of "A" and "B" together making sure that "C" and "D" are not sewn into the seam. When all seams are stitched, knotted and excess sinew removed, turn the pouch inside-out. Carefully work all of the corners out so that the pouch will lie flat.

(10) Finally, cut the fringe in "C" and "D" by making cuts that are about 1/8" in width (**Figure 5**).

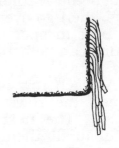

HINTS

(**A**) Rosettes done directly on leather will always bunch up unless a material such as lightweight paper sacking or canvas is tacked onto the back of the leather being used. This creates extra tension and, therefore, a flat pattern will develop.

Figure 5

(**B**) The spot stitch used in this project may be done with one needle. Simply follow the guidelines given but use just one needle.

(**C**) Take your time as you put the project together. If you want to make any changes in the pouch size or the beading pattern, etc., plot how to make them part of the finished project.

(**D**) The imitation sinew will be easier to use and still be strong enough if it is split into three or four sewing "threads."

(**E**) When the pouch is beaded, it is suggested that the smooth side of the leather be on the outside if you desire a finished look. If the rough or suede side is exposed, however, the pouch will have a more rustic or "primitive" look.

(**F**) A thong may be sewn on the back if desired.

(**G**) When making your rosettes, be sure that they are constructed as a circle within a circle and not as a spiral as this would throw your spacing off.

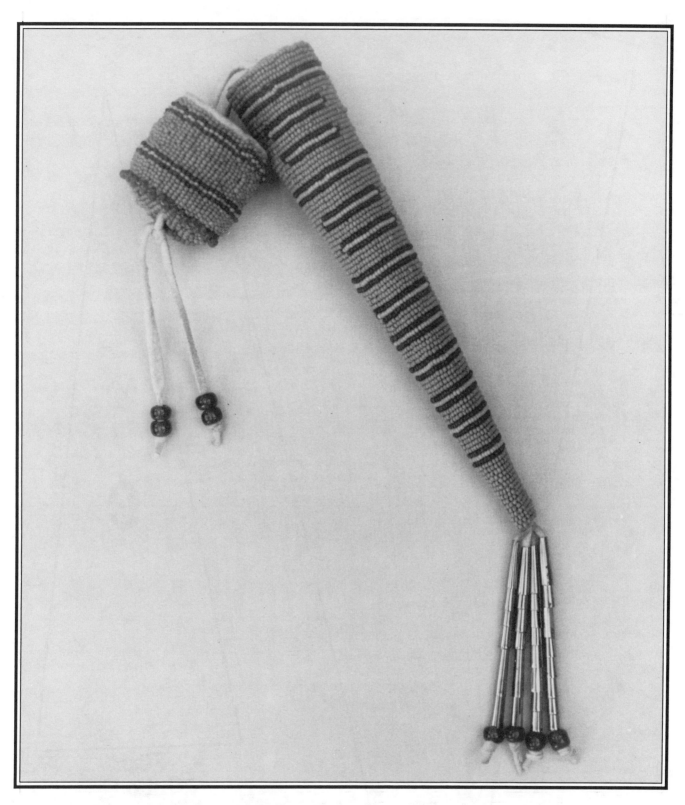

BEADED AWL CASE (Return Stitch)

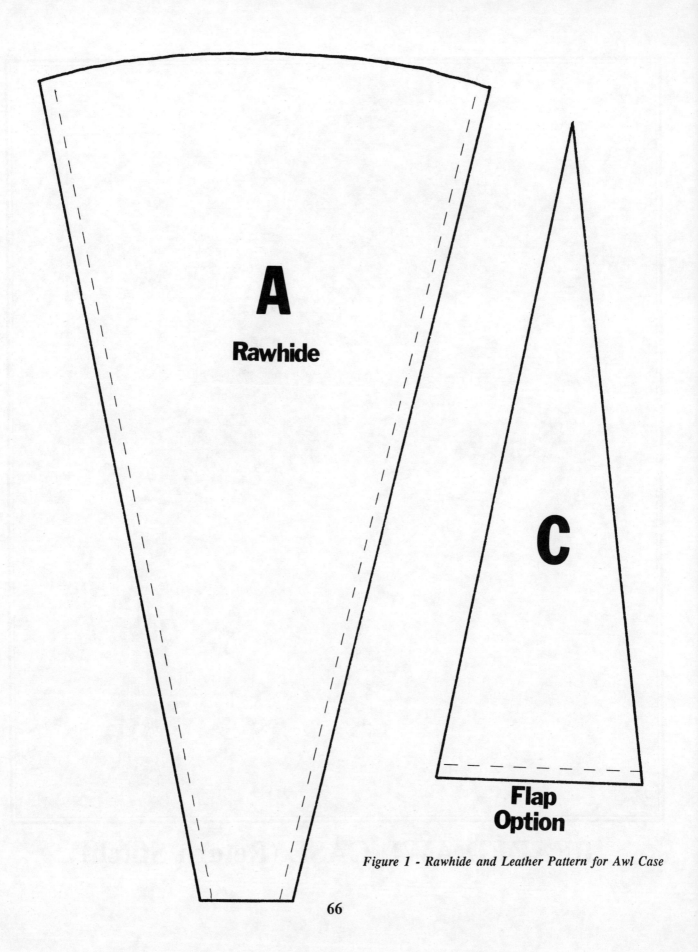

A

Rawhide

C

Flap Option

Figure 1 - Rawhide and Leather Pattern for Awl Case

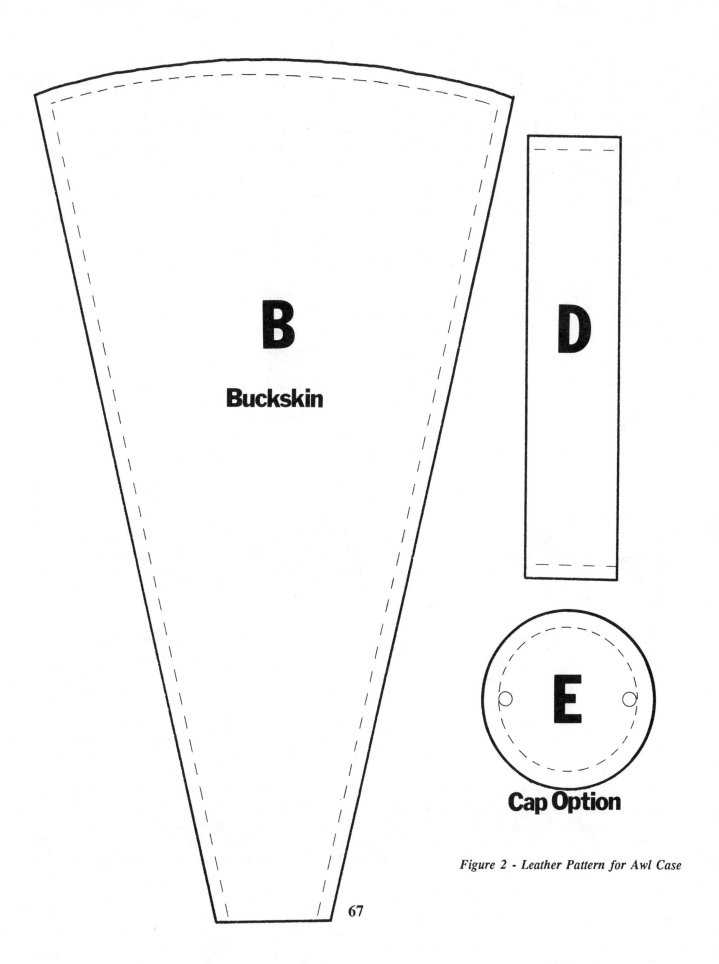

B

Buckskin

D

E

Cap Option

67

Figure 2 - Leather Pattern for Awl Case

The awl was one of the most useful, and therefore important, tools owned by an Indian woman as it was used in much of the craftwork of the Tribe. Therefore, the *Beaded Awl Case* was likewise important as it was a handy container to hold and protect the awl. The techniques introduced in this project are also important to the student of American Indian craftwork as they are used in a wide variety of projects such as the bonnet case and many others. The "inside-out" stitch will also be of great use in many Indian items.

It should be noted that if you are making an awl case for a particular awl, the dimensions of this case should be tailored to your specific needs using the same techniques as directed.

MATERIALS NEEDED

1   Piece thin rawhide 5" x 9"
1   Piece buckskin 4 1/2" x 7 1/4"
2   Feet imitation sinew
1   #8 Glover's or leather needle
1   Bobbin "A" nymo thread
1   #11 Sharp beading needle
1   Piece beeswax
4   Oz. 10/° blue seed beads
2   Oz. 10/° yellow seed beads
2   Oz. 10/° red seed beads

(1) From the rawhide piece, cut out the awl case body following the pattern. Then, using an awl or other sharp instrument (Be Careful), punch stitch holes about 1/8" from the top that are spaced 1/8" apart. Then make similar stitch holes down each side. These holes will be used to sew the awl sides together, so make sure they are uniform and matching.

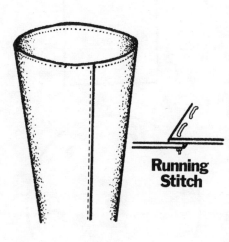

Running Stitch

Figure 3

(2) Now roll the rawhide to form a triangular shaped cone with the sides overlapping each other by about 1/4" (and so that the holes are overlapping and matching). To make sewing easier, you may want to put a small, single stitch at the top and one at the bottom - these are temporary and this technique is called "tacking." With the imitation sinew, sew the case together as shown in **Figure 3**.

(3) Follow the pattern and cut out Leather Piece "B". (This is a very important step, so take your time and make sure that the leather fits just right.) Wrap the leather around the rawhide so that it is snug, the top is even with the top of the rawhide top and the sides almost touch each other. Tack the leather in place as you trim and adjust it as needed. Be sure that you have it adjusted "just right" before going to the next step.

(4) Split the imitation sinew into three or four sewing threads and, using the inside-out stitch (**Figure 4**), start at the top of the leather and sew it into place creating a snug fit over the rawhide. The leather will have a certain amount of "give" or "stretch" to it and this stitch is used to pull the sides together without putting too much stress on the inner rawhide cone. Any tacking can, of course, be taken out as you progress with the sewing of the seam down the case.

(5) Finally, as shown in **Figure 5**, use a whip stitch and attach the leather to the rawhide at the top of the awl case using the pre-punched holes as a guide.

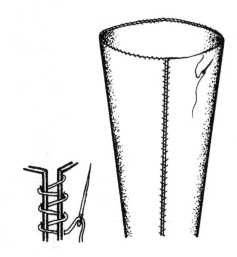

Figure 4   *Figure 5*

You may use either of the options given for the top of the awl case and patterns have been provided to do either of these:

(6) To use the Awl Case Flap, cut the flap from the leather pattern given and sew this to the top back of the awl case as shown in **Figure 6**. The flap should fall to the front of the awl case and dangles or beading on the end of the flap are a common decoration that will help hold it over the front.

(7) The other option is for the Leather Awl Case Cap. This is a bit more difficult to make but start by cutting the cap piece out of the leather following the pattern. Please note that if the awl case is going to be beaded, make the cap piece 1/4" larger than shown so that it will fit over the beads.

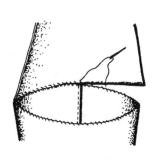

Figure 6

Figure 7

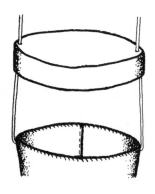

(8) Stitch the seams of the awl cap side "D" together to form a circle. Then whip stitch the seams of awl cap lid "E" to the top of piece "D". Attach two (2) 6" leather thongs to the top of the awl case at the sides leaving the ends free. Finally, punch holes in the awl lid and slip the thongs through, creating a removable lid for your awl case (**Figure 7**). These thongs may be attached to your belt. Thongs may be attached, of course, even if you use the awl case flap option.

If the awl case is to be beaded, the awl case is

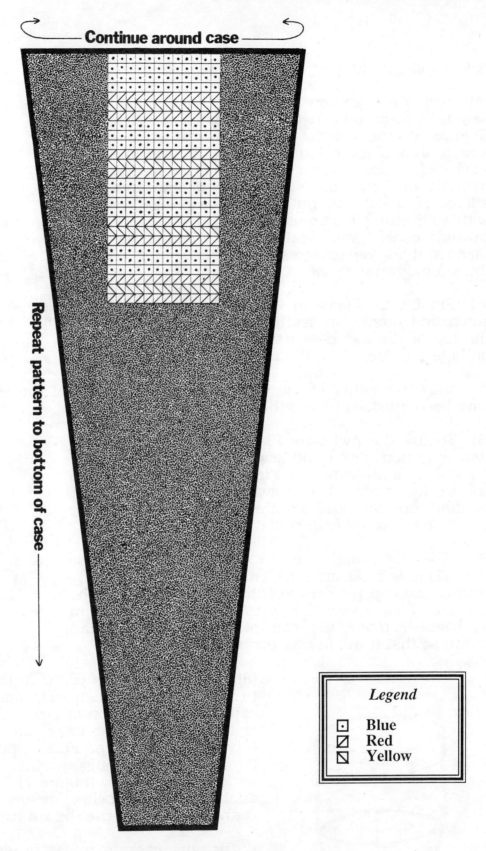

Figure 8 - Beading Pattern for awl case

70

not complete. In order to bead it, follow the remaining instructions:

(9) The beading technique that will be used in this project is a variation of the *Return Stitch* and, as shown in this book, it is not only useful on round objects, but may be used on any item requiring an applique stitch like the running stitch.

(10) Begin by cutting off a comfortable length (about 24") from the bobbin of nymo thread and threading about 6" through one of the beading needles. In the end of the long (18") end of the thread make a good secure knot - this is done so that you can pull the thread through the needle as the work progresses and so that there will be only one strand of thread through each bead. Then drag the thread across the beeswax so that it is covered with wax.

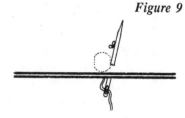

(11) From the outside of the leather at about 1/2" from the bottom of the awl case, push the needle with the thread into the leather, take it down to about 1/2 bead length from the bottom and push the tip of the needle out of the leather (**Figure 9**). Pull the needle and the thread through the leather.

(12) String five (5) beads onto the needle and thread, hold the beads next to the awl case leather and, even with the last bead, take the needle back into the leather pointing back towards the beads. *Figure 10* Bring the needle back up through the leather even with the second to last bead (**Figure 10**) and pull the needle and thread through completely holding the beads snug (not too tight). The nice thing about this stitch is that the rawhide backing will allow you to "slide" the point of the needle against it and help you guide the needle to the proper place; never allow the needle to go through the rawhide.

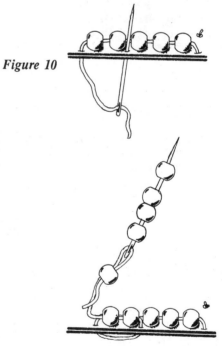

(13) Now thread the needle through the last two beads in the row, string five more beads onto the needle and thread and, even with the last bead, take the needle back into the leather pointing back towards the beads. Bring the needle back up through the leather even with the second to last bead and pull the needle and thread through completely holding the beads tightly in place - and so forth around the awl case as shown in **Figure 11**.

Figure 11

If you use the possible beading pattern enclosed, the first beads to go on the awl case will be red. After a row of red, then yellow, then a row of red and then three rows of blue. It is most difficult to draw a beading pattern for a round object as the number of beads in each row will differ depending upon how big around the object is and, of course, that will change as you move up the awl case. So keep this in mind and use the pattern as a guide only.

(14) Continue beading up the case with the return stitch as described in Step 13, keeping the rows uniformly next to each other, until you reach the top of the awl case. *NOTE*: As you bead your way up the awl case you will pass over the first knot that was made to secure your thread to the awl leather; be sure that the excess thread is cut off and that you hide the knot with the beading. Further, if you have to add more beading thread to your needle as the project progresses, do it in the same manner taking care to hide the knot with the beading.

(15) To tie off the beads you simply do a series of three return stitches in this manner: Go back under three beads (instead of two), bring the needle through the leather and take it back through two beads. Then go back under the leather a distance of five beads, come up through the leather and go back through two beads, then back into the leather and back five beads and up through the leather behind the fifth bead (this will be the ninth bead from the end of the last row). It is important to keep your beading thread waxed during the beading, but at this stage re-wax the thread and then take the needle and thread through all nine beads, pull the thread tight and cut it off. This will hold the beads in place without an additional knot. **Figure 12** shows how to do this final step; for clarity it is drawn on a flat surface, whereas you will be beading this on the round awl case.

Figure 12

HINTS

(A) Take your time as you create the awl case. As with most craftwork, the greater effort put into this project, the nicer the finished project will be.

(B) The imitation sinew may be used full strength but it is easier to use if it is split into pieces. For this project it might be a good idea to split it into two (2) pieces for the sewing of the rawhide and into three or four pieces for the leather work.

(C) The seam made by the two ends of the rawhide coming together does not have to be in the same position as the place where the two ends of the leather are sewn together. It may be, in fact, easier to do the inside-out stitch if the leather is sewn at a different point on the awl case.

(D) The leather may be beaded before sewing the case together but it is much easier to do this beading after the leather has been sewn to the rawhide and it will hide all of the seams, etc. Further, the beading may be done with a "running stitch" (described in this book) instead of the return stitch if you so desire.

(E) As mentioned before, the step that will make the whole awl case look very good or very bad is in adjusting the leather and sewing it in place over the rawhide. Be sure and take enough time to insure that this is done correctly.

(F) Dangles with tin cones, bells or whatever may be added to the bottom of the awl case if you want to add them. If this is the case, be sure that all of this is done before the case is beaded as the rows will hide any knots that might be necessary.

NOTES

QUILLED PIPE BAG (Quill Wrapping)

75

Of all the possessions of the American Indian the pipe was the one that was held most dearly. Used both in ceremonials and for pleasure, all pipes, with the exception of the "elbow pipe," were the exclusive domain of the man. Often, the *Quilled Pipe Bag* was one of the most elaborately decorated items owned by a warrior as it protected his most prized ceremonial pipe.

This project may be beaded and enclosed is a possible beading pattern, but specific beading instructions have not been included. It is fairly easy to adapt the beading instructions from other projects in this book and, because of the style of this pipe bag, it is suggested that a lazy stitch technique be used.

MATERIALS NEEDED

3 Pkgs natural quills
5 Pkgs dyed quills
2 Pieces buckskin 24" x 5"
1 Piece buckskin 9 1/2" x 8"
1 Piece rawhide 4 3/4" x 5"
2 Feet imitation sinew
1 #8 Glover's or leather needle
4 Oz. 11/° white seed beads*
1 Oz. 11/° red seed beads*
1 Oz. 11/° light blue seed beads*
1 Oz. 11/° dark blue seed beads*
1 #12 Sharps beading needle*
2 Bobbins "A" nymo thread*
1 Piece beeswax*

(*) Needed only if the bag is to be beaded.

-- Preparing the Bag --

(1) Using the buckskin, cut two (2) pieces that measure 5" x 24" (these will make the front and back of the pipe bag), one (1) rawhide piece that is 4 3/4" by 5" and one (1) piece of buckskin that measures 9 1/2" x 8" for the fringe piece at the bottom. *NOTE:* If you are making this pipe bag for a particular pipe you will want to measure the pipe and cut the leather pieces accordingly. Keep in mind that the bag should be "roomy" and that you should allow an additional 6" at the top for the "flap."

(2) Keeping in mind that the pouch will be turned inside-out after sewing, place the "front" leather piece on a flat surface (such as a table). Now lay the rawhide piece in the center of the front piece so that there is 1/8" showing on both sides. Then lay the back piece on top of these two so that it matches the front piece exactly as shown in **Figure 1**. *NOTE:* If you are going to bead or quill the front or back (on pipe bags, usually both front and back were beaded), this should be done before this step. Further, you should insure that the beading is inside of the bag before sewing and be very careful when the bag is pulled inside-out to insure that none of the beading is injured.

(3) Split the imitation sinew into three or four threads and put one of these on the Glover's (leather-type) needle. Make a good secure knot in one end of the imitation sinew.

(4) Making sure that the leather pieces do not move and starting at the middle of what will be the bottom, use the simple running stitch (**Figures 1 & 2**) and sew the three (3) pieces together. You will want to stop sewing when you reach the top of the side; make a knot and cut off the excess imitation sinew. Do Not sew the other end closed as this will be the top of the bag. Also, be sure that you Do Not catch the rawhide piece with the needle and imitation sinew when you are sewing up the sides of the front and back pieces.

(5) Making sure that the rawhide piece has not changed position and using another thread of imitation sinew, start again at the middle of the bottom and sew the rest of the bottom and the other side together. Make a good knot and cut off the excess imitation sinew at the top corner of the bag. Then, carefully turn the bag inside-out so that the sewing is hidden and the rawhide piece hangs down.

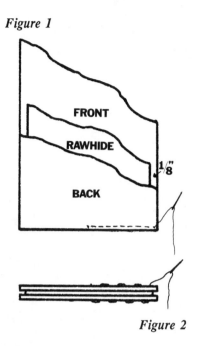

Figure 1

Figure 2

- - Rawhide Preparation - -

(6) Section the rawhide by drawing lines every 3/16" across the entire width of the piece vertically (**Figure 3**). Then draw your pattern on the rawhide where designs and colors will be and an additional line about 1/8" from the bottom edge to mark where the quill work will stop. These lines should be light enough so that none of them will show through the quills when the bag is finished.

(7) Using a razor, craft knife or sharp scissors (Be Careful), cut the 3/16" strips from the bottom of the rawhide piece to the bottom of the bag. Make these cuts as straight as possible!

(8) The bag is now ready for quilling.

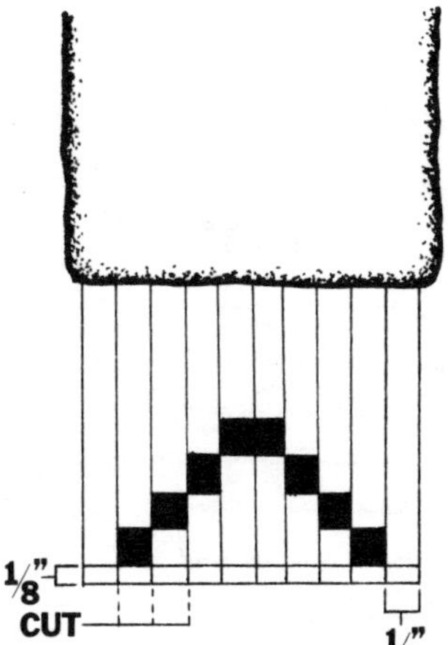

Figure 3

- - Quill Preparation - -

(9) From the quills that are available, choose those that are thin and 2 inches or longer. Wash these quills in hot, soapy water until they are all clean of any natural oils. If you have to dye your own quills, this should be done at this stage and is

77

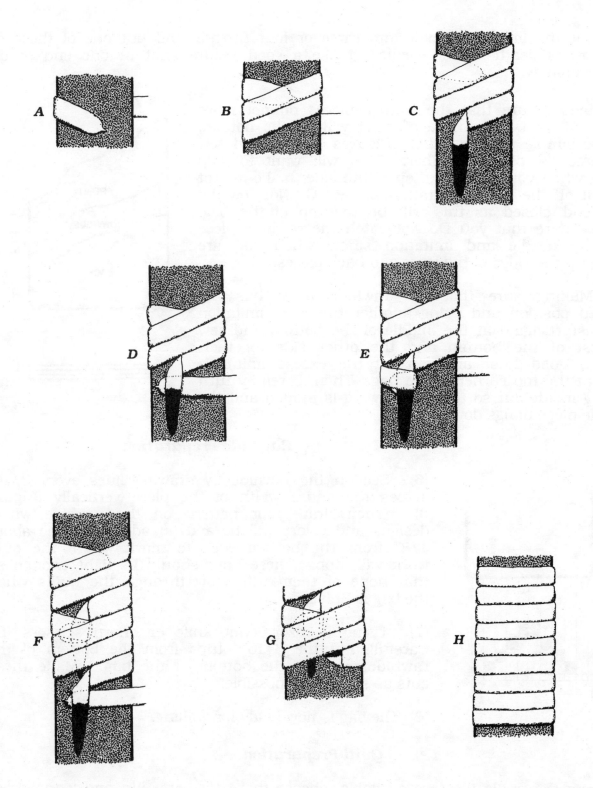

Figure 4 - Quill Wrapping Technique

78

relatively easy if you use any organic dye with just a drop of vinegar or lemon oil to set the color.

(10)   Quills must be softened before using them in the wrapping technique. Traditionally, the quill worker would place the quills in her mouth and allow the saliva to soften the quills. This is very dangerous and we cannot recommend it! A method that will work well is to have a small bowl of water with the quills that will be used in it and this container may be placed in front of you as you work.

- - Quilling the Rawhide - -

(11)   The technique for using quills is shown in **Figure 4a** through **Figure 4h**. Using a softened quill (these will become hard again after you wrap them as they become dry), you want to make it flat. This may be done by holding the quill on the table and pressing down with your thumb nail across it or by using a dull knife in place of your thumb nail. Now, hold the rounded end (or bottom) of the quill against the top of the first rawhide 1/4" strip with your left hand; make sure that the front of the bag is facing away from you. The quill should be pointed with the black, pointed end up toward the bag and slightly to the left. Then, holding the bottom in position, wrap the quill to the left (**Figure 4a**), making sure not to twist it, and wrap it completely around the rawhide strip. Continue around and over the bottom of the quill holding it in place. There may be a small amount of twisting of the rounded tip to accomplish this, but keep it to the very minimum (**Figure 4b**).

(12)   Continue wrapping the quill around the rawhide until you get to the black area at the point, or top. The black part of the quill should not show on the front of the strip and when this area is reached stop wrapping and make a downward twist of the quill tip, laying the tip along the center of the strip with the point going down the strip. To do this (**Figure 4c**), make a "groove" with your finger nail at about a 45° angle on the quill and fold it over itself with the tip pointing down.

(13)   Using your left hand, hold the wrapped quill in place and, with your right hand, insert the rounded bottom of a new softened quill under the twist of the previous quill (**Figure 4d**). Fold this quill to the left, over the point of the first quill (**Figure 4e**), and repeat the wrapping (*Step 11* and *Step 12*) making sure that the point is held securely under the wrapping; cover all of the exposed black tips as you wrap down the piece. Continue down the rawhide making sure that each successive wrap is as close to the previous wrap as possible to make sure that the rawhide does not show on the front and that both the top and bottom of the last quill are securely covered (wrapped) on the back. (**Figure 4f**)

(14)   The first couple of quills are sometimes difficult to start but the others will begin to lay in without any trouble as the work progresses. Continue to wrap the rawhide until the line drawn in *Step Six* at the bottom of the piece has been reached. At this point twist the black tip up under the quill wrapping, pull or push it into place and let it set to dry as shown in **Figure 4g**. The front of the quilled rawhide is shown in **Figure 4h**.

Figure 5

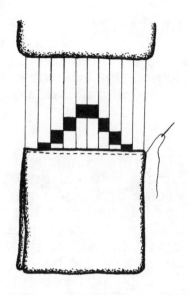

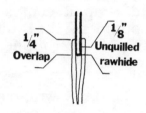

(**15**) The final step is to add the fringe piece in *Step 1* to the bottom of the quilled rawhide piece. As shown in **Figure 5**, the fringe piece is wrapped around the bottom of the rawhide strip and sewn, with a running stitch, into place. The top of the leather will be about 1/4" above the bottom of the rawhide and will cover and protect the bottom of the quillwork (it will also hide any mistakes that may have been made in the bottom wrap). After it is secured in place, cut fringe of 1/4" or less in width all the way around as shown in **Figure 6**.

HINTS

The instructions included above will allow you to make a very nice *Quilled Pipe Bag* and the following information is presented here to make it easier to accomplish.

(**A**) If the pouch is to be beaded or quilled, this may be done before sewing the pouch together as explained in *Steps 2* through *4*.

(**B**) The imitation sinew will work best and still be very strong if it is split into three or four "threads."

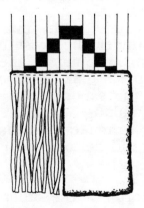

(**C**) While doing quillwork is not the easiest craft to do correctly, it is not as hard as most people believe and many good quill workers maintain that it is as easy and fast as beadwork after the basics have been mastered. However, for the beginning craftsperson it is an excellent idea to practice the basic wrapping technique explained in *Step 11* and *Step 12* before starting a large project. You may want to make a 1/4" wide rawhide strip and practice this technique before getting into quilling this bag.

(**D**) The best source of instructions available at this time is **The Techniques of Porcupine Quill Decoration Among the Indians of North America** by Wm. C. Orchard. A copy of this book will reveal the following information that may be helpful on other quill projects: (**1**) Various ways to do quill work are explained throughout the book but the technique used in this project is described and illustrated on page 19. (**2**) Various sources of dyes that may be

Figure 6

used on quills are described on pages 9-14. **(3)** On pages 14-15, Orchard describes and explains the various tools that may be used in quill work. These tools are pictured on pages 12-13.

(E) To accomplish *Step 15*, the quilled strips may have to be joined together at the bottom with stitching or masking tape before they can be sewn to the fringe piece.

(F) Some quill workers prefer to cut the rawhide "strips" leaving a 1/4" area at the bottom and top of the rawhide uncut. This is probably a bit more difficult when quilling as the "strips" are not completely separate, but it will make it much easier to sew the fringe piece into place as the strips are in one piece. If you use this technique, the strips should be quilled before the pouch is sewn together (*Step 4*).

(G) Further, some craftspersons prefer to quill the rawhide first and then sew the back and rawhide together (*Step 4*).

(H) In any event, please note that the quills must not be too wet before doing the quill wrapping technique as excessive moisture will distort the shape of the rawhide that is being worked.

(I) The most important "*Hint*" that can be given regarding most craft work, and particularly for quillwork, is to take your time and do not rush the project. When you finish quilling one strip, for example, wait for five or ten minutes before starting the next one, etc.

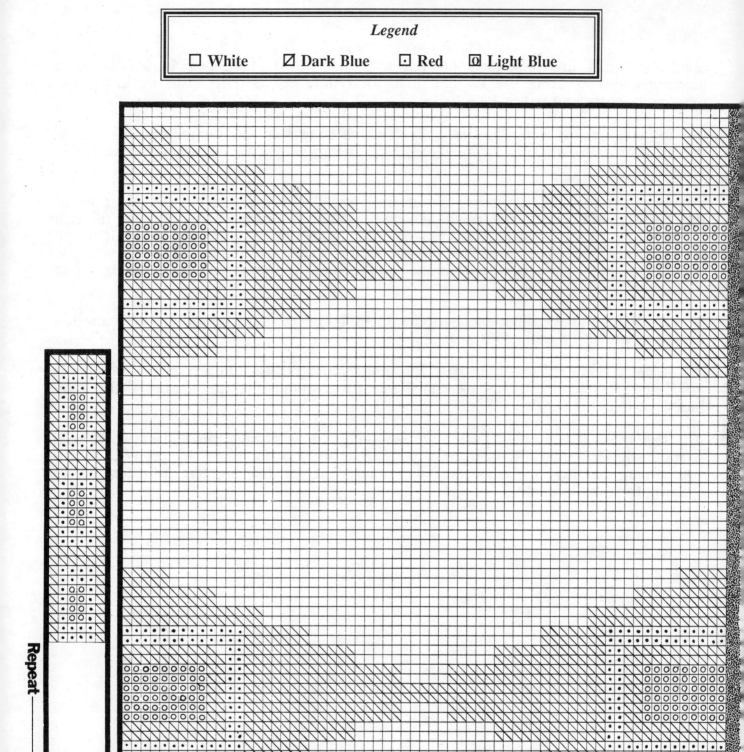

Repeat

Figure 7 - Possible Beading Pattern for Quilled Pipe Bag

82

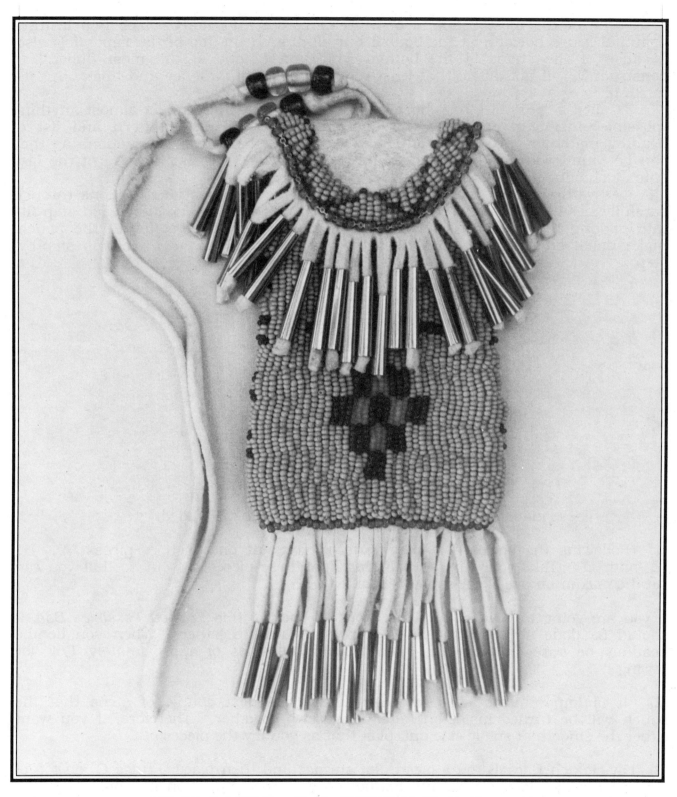

FRINGED POSSIBLES BAG

One of the most beautiful of containers, the *Fringed Possibles Bag* features beautiful fringe not only at the bottom but all around the top of the flap. It is also, because of the shape of the bottom fringe piece, one of the most difficult to construct . . . if not difficult, at least requiring a lot of patience and time. But it's worth it.

Called a "possibles bag" because you could carry and protect almost anything "possible" inside of one, you will find enclosed a beading pattern and list of beading materials. We have not, however, included beading instructions as they can be found within other projects in this book. We suggest the use of the lazy stitch technique if you choose to bead this attractive bag.

As with all craft projects, we suggest that you read the instructions through carefully before beginning construction so that you understand how each step fits into making the item. If you would like to change or "personalize" the pouch, make notes on where this will be done and then follow the directions step-by-step.

MATERIALS NEEDED

1 Piece buckskin 5" x 5 1/2"
1 Piece buckskin 7" x 7"
2 Feet imitation sinew
1 #8 Glover's or leather needle
1 Bobbin "A" thread*
2 #11 Sharps beading needle*
1 Piece beeswax*
5 Oz. 10/° red seed beads*
1 Oz. 10/° yellow seed beads*
1 Oz. 10/° green seed beads*

(*) These materials are needed only if the bag is to be beaded.

(1) Following the enclosed leather patterns, cut out one each of pieces "A", "B", "C" and "D". Take your time in planning how these pieces are cut so that you can get the maximum use of the available leather.

If you are going to bead or quill the front or back of this *Fringed Possibles Bag*, it should be done at this stage and before it is sewn together. When you do the beading, be sure and leave an area around the sides of approximately 1/4" for sewing.

(2) It is important to keep in mind during the next couple of steps that the pouch will be turned inside-out after it is sewn together. Therefore, if you want either the smooth or suede side out, plan that as you lay the pieces out.

(3) Lay "Pouch Back B" on a clean, flat surface and then place "Fringe C" on top of it matching the dots, circles and bottom seam. Then put "Pouch Front A" on top of these two pieces so that the bottoms are all even. Strip the imitation sinew into three or four sewing threads and place one of these on the leather needle.

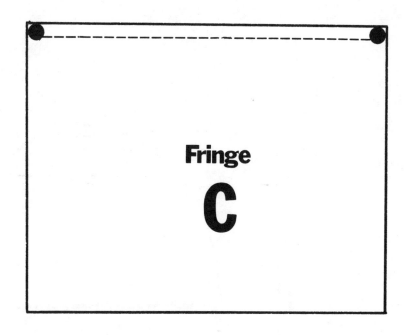

Fringe

C

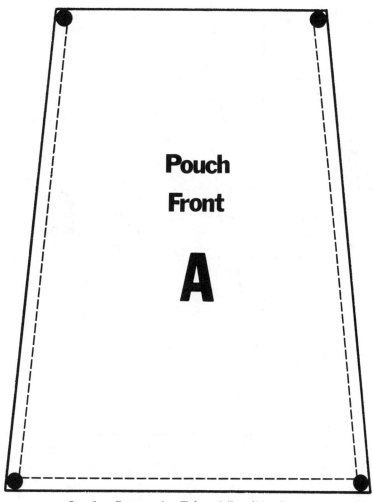

Pouch

Front

A

Leather Pattern for Fringed Possibles Bag

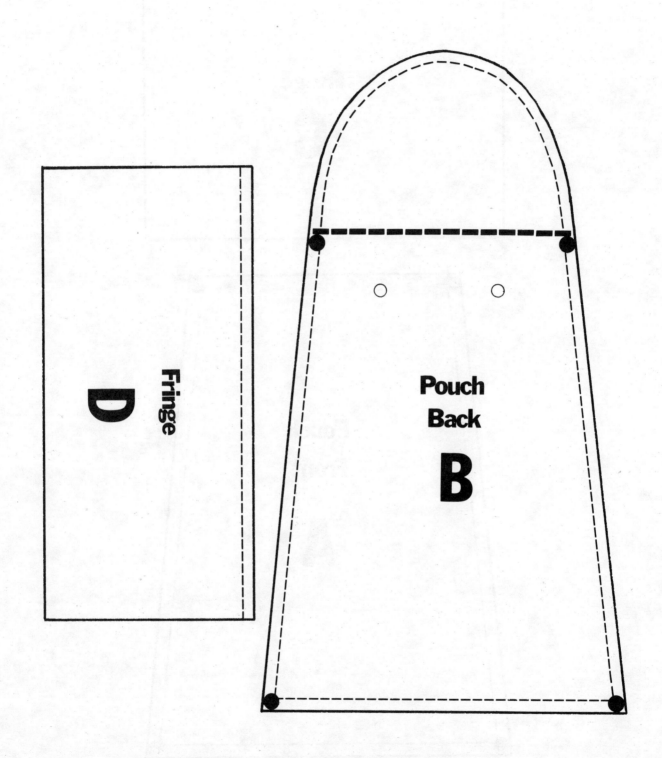

Leather Pattern for Fringed Possibles Bag

Now, making sure that none of the leather pieces move, use a running stitch and sew them together at the bottom as shown in **Figure 1**.

(4) Next you want to start at the bottom right-hand corner, with another thread of sinew, and sew up the right sides of "A" and "B" together. This is the most difficult part of the sewing as you Do Not want to catch the fringe piece "C" in the stitching. This requires that you pull the top part of "C" in and out of the way as you stitch the right side. At the top corner of "A" make a secure, neat knot and cut off the excess imitation sinew. Then, insuring that "C" is not caught in the seam, repeat this procedure on the left side. As will now become evident, it is very important that the fringe piece "C" does not become part of the sewing on either side.

(5) Turn the pouch inside-out so that the fringe piece hangs down and all of the side stitching is hidden. If all is well, proceed to the next step.

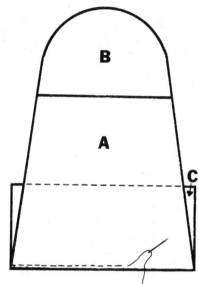

Figure 1

Figure 2

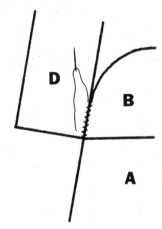

(6) As shown in **Figure 2**, use a whip stitch and sew "Fringe D" to the top of "Pouch B" starting at the left fold line and continuing around to the right fold line. Neither of the pieces of leather overlap one another, but meet "side to side." Do not worry about the shape that "D" assumes during the sewing as when the fringe is cut, this piece will lay flat.

(7) Finally, cut the fringe in "C" and "D" by making cuts that are about 1/8" in width as shown in **Figure 3**. Take your time with this and make sure that the fringe is even and uniform in width.

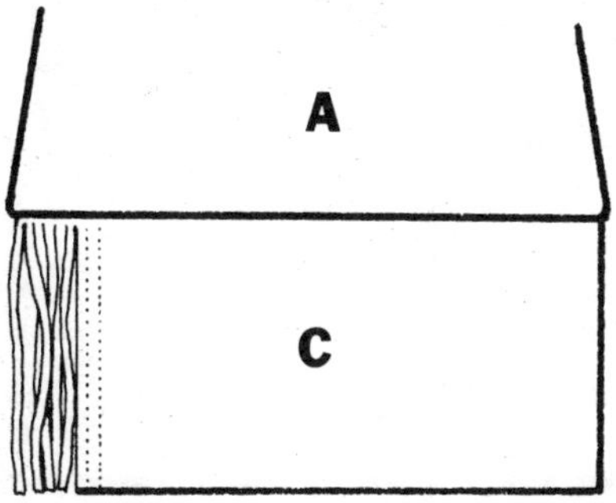

HINTS

(A) Be sure and take your time as you put the bag together. Any changes that you want to make should be incorporated into the instructions as you proceed.

(B) "Tie strings" may be added at the back of the bag, if desired.

(C) For complete beading instructions, consult the techniques described in this book for the various methods. All are listed in the *Table of Contents*.

Figure 3

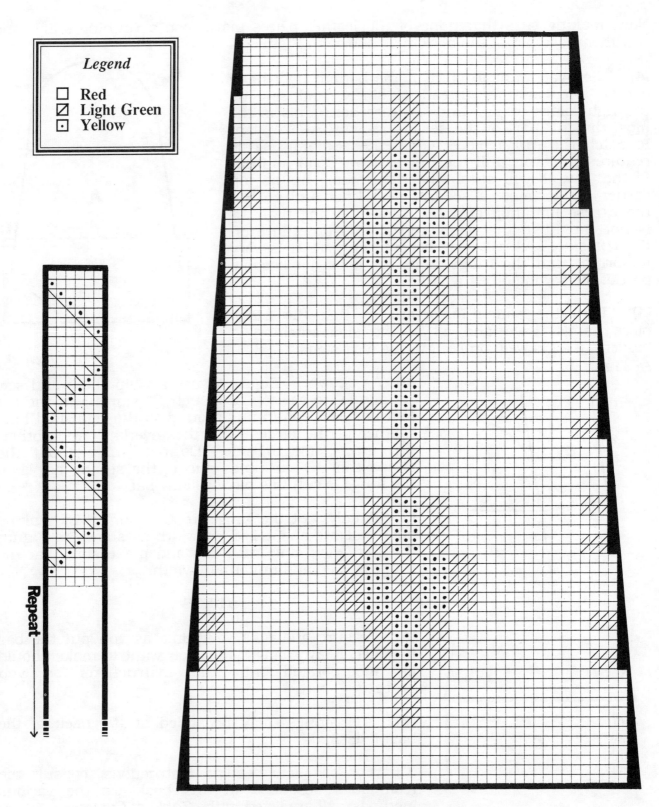

Possible Beading Pattern for Fringed Possibles Bag

FRINGED MIRROR POUCH

The *Fringed Mirror Pouch* is one of the most attractive pouches because of the fringe that completely surrounds the finished project. It may, of course, be made to hold almost any small item, but the mirror was a very special piece of equipment to the Indian and was often traded for a wealth of hides or furs. Included is a possible beading pattern and suggested materials but we have not included beading instructions. The beading pattern may be done using either a lazy stitch or running stitch, but the beginning bead worker will find the running stitch easier because of the curved bottom. Complete instructions may be adapted from any of the other projects in this book.

MATERIALS NEEDED

1 Buckskin piece 4" x 16"
1 Buckskin piece 12 1/4" x 2"
2 Feet imitation sinew
1 #8 Glover's or leather needle
1 Bobbin "A" nymo thread*
1 #11 Sharps beading needle*
1 Piece beeswax*
3 Oz. 11/° white seed beads*
2 Oz. 11/° blue seed beads*
2 Oz. 11/° red seed beads*

(*) Needed only if the pouch is to be beaded.

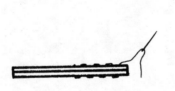

Figure 1

(1) Following the enclosed pattern, cut out the two pieces of leather ("A" and "B"). In addition to these, the pouch fringe piece, or "C"' should be made to measure exactly 12 3/4" x 2"; you will note that the pattern is too large for the book pages and is shown in two parts. Make sure that you plan your cutting so that all three pieces may be cut from a minimum amount of leather.

(2) Keeping in mind that the pouch will be turned inside-out after it is sewn together, place "Pouch A" on top of "Pouch Back B" matching the dots and circles and the outside seams. With the imitation sinew, start in the middle of the bottom and, making sure the pieces remain in place, sew along the bottom and up the right side to the top of "Pouch A" and "fold" line on "B" (see **Figure 1**). Make a good knot and cut off the excess thread. *NOTE*: If the pouch is to be painted, beaded or quilled this should be done prior to this step.

Leather Pattern for Fringed Mirror Pouch

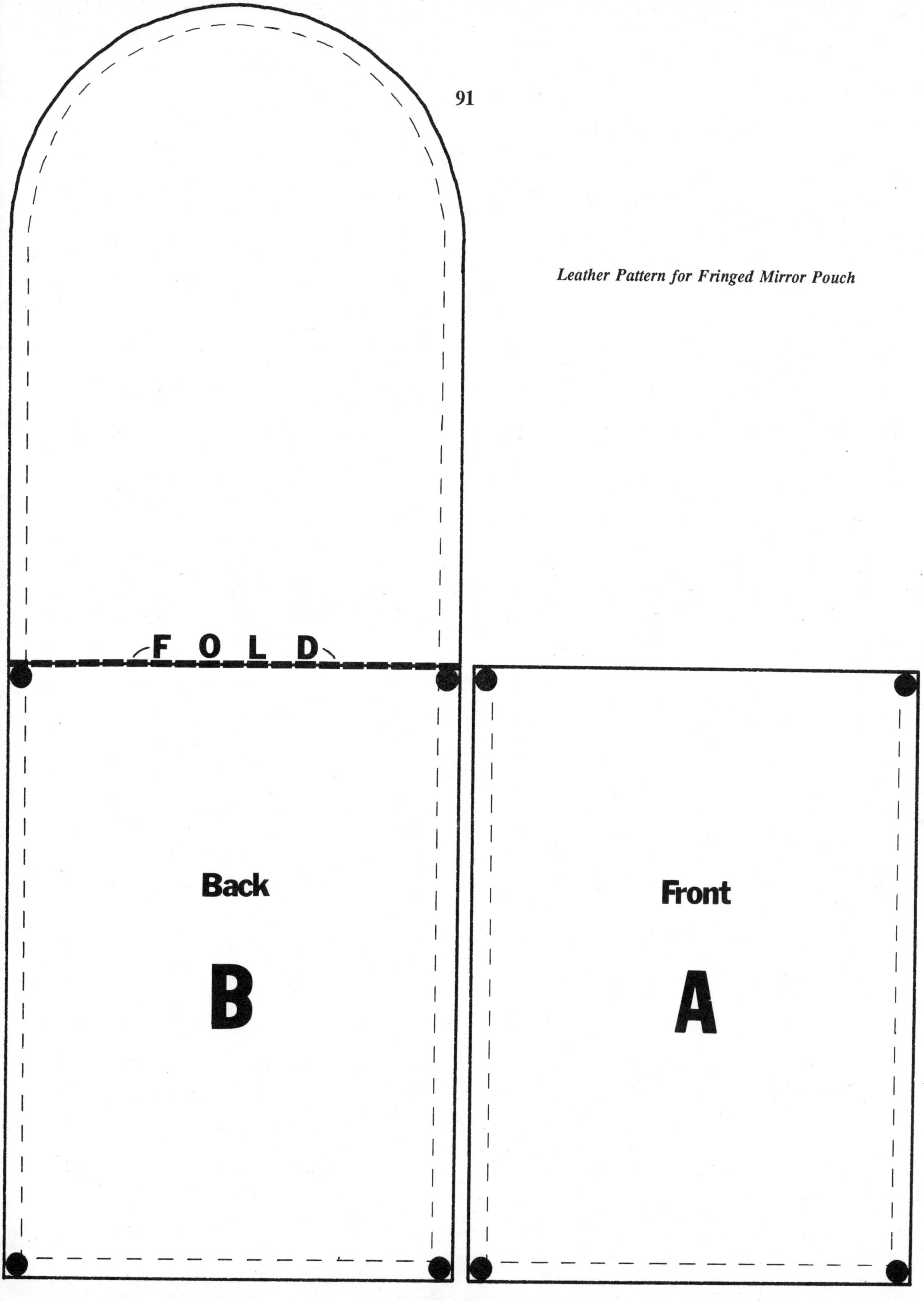

F O L D

Back

B

Front

A

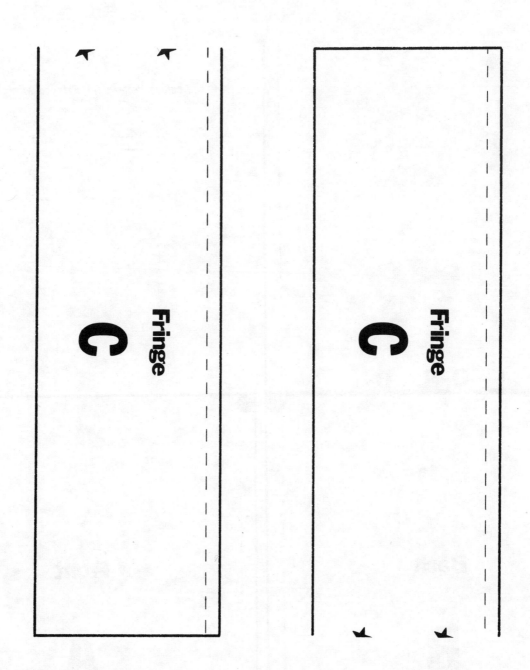

Leather Pattern for Fringed Mirror Pouch - Fringe Piece

(3) Go back to the middle of the bottom and, using another piece of imitation sinew, sew from there up the left side to the fold line. Make a good knot and cut off the excess sinew.

(4) Now turn the pouch inside-out and carefully work the corners out so that the bag lies flat.

(5) With a whip stitch, sew "Fringe C" to the top of "Pouch B" starting at the left fold line and continuing around to the right fold line (**Figure 2**). Do not worry about the shape that "C" assumes during the sewing as it will lay flat after the fringe has been cut; wait, however, until it is sewn in place before cutting fringe or it will be in your way.

(6) Finally, as shown in **Figure 3**, cut the fringe in "C" by making cuts that are about 1/8" in width. Make these as uniform as possible.

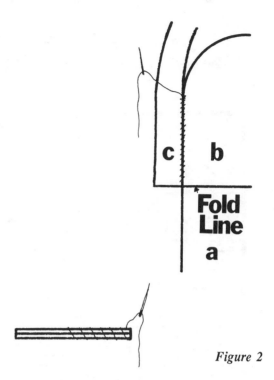

Figure 2

HINTS

(A) Take your time as you put the project together. If you want to make any changes, plot how to make them part of the finished project before you start.

(B) The imitation sinew will work much better if it is split into three or four sewing "threads." This will also make it much easier to thread the needle.

(C) "Tie strings" may be added to the back of the pouch if desired.

(D) As noted in the instructions, any beading or quilling that is desired should be done before the pouch is sewn together.

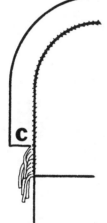

Figure 3

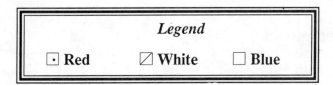

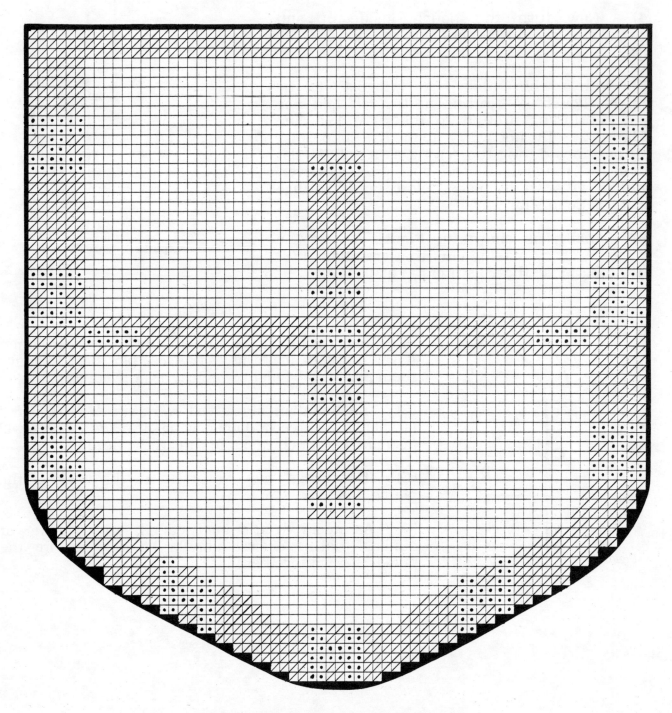

Possible Beading Pattern for Fringed Mirror Pouch

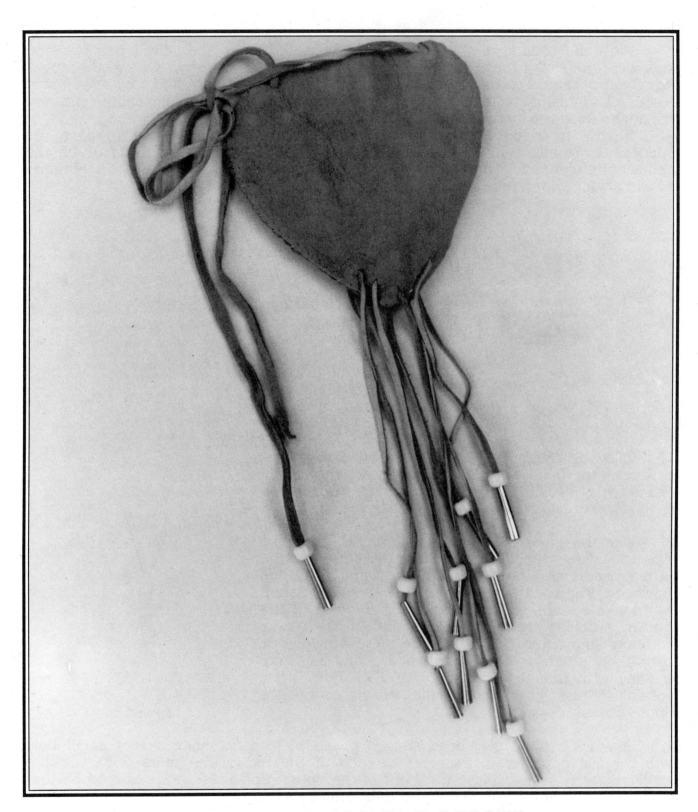

GAGE d'MORE POUCH

95

With the coming of the fur traders the numbers of specialized pouches and bags were increased to fit the life-style of these fascinating men. One of these was the *Gage d'More Pouch*, which was used to hold tobacco and the clay pipe. Described in historical text, this pouch was used not only by the white man but was adapted for use by the Indian as well.

If you are making a traditional-style pouch it will look best to have the "suede," or rough side of the leather showing. Be sure to read all of the instructions completely before starting and this project will include the technique of bead edging with a number of possible variations as described earlier.

MATERIALS NEEDED

2	Pieces buckskin 5 1/2" x 8 1/2"
1	Piece buckskin 1 1/4" x 12"
2	Yards imitation sinew
1	#8 Glover's or leather needle
10	Glass crow beads
10	Medium tin cones
2	Oz. 10/° white seed beads
2	Oz. 10/° dark blue seed beads
1	#11 Sharps beading needles
1	Piece beeswax
1	Bobbin "D" nymo thread

(1) Following the patterns enclosed, cut two pieces of buckskin following the outline for the small tobacco bag ("A") and two pieces using the pattern for the larger bag ("B").

(2) Take the imitation sinew and split it into three or four sewing threads. Place one of these on the leather needle and, using a simple running stitch (as shown in **Figure 1**), sew together the small pouch "A". Make certain that the beginning and end of the running stitch is securely knotted, cut off the excess imitation sinew and then turn the pouch inside-out so that the stitching is hidden inside. This bag may be filled with tobacco or may be used to hold other "possibles" and is stored inside the larger (*Gage d'More*) Pouch.

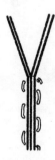

Figure 1

(3) On one of the larger, heart-shaped pieces of leather, make a very small hole (with an awl or other instrument) at each of the ten places marked "X" on the leather pattern. This will be the front of the pouch and these holes should be just big enough to string a 1/8" thong through - no larger!

96

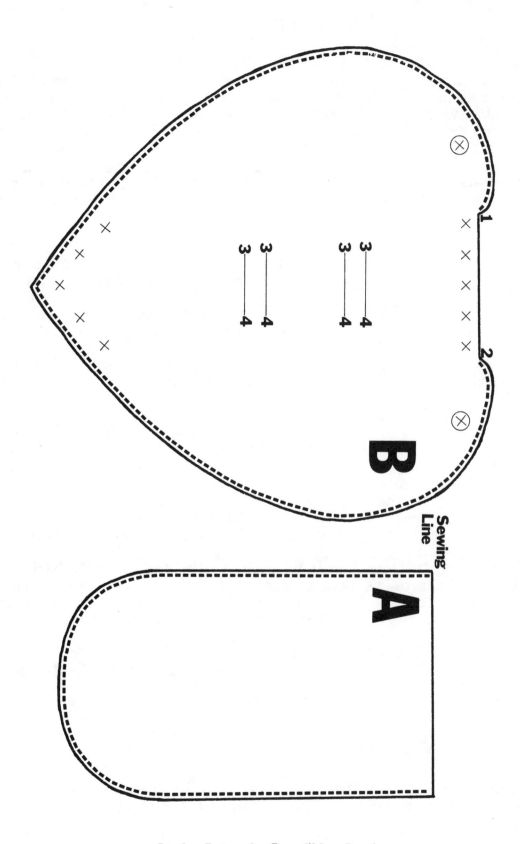

Leather Pattern for Gage d'More Pouch

97

(4)   Keeping in mind that you will turn the pouch inside-out after sewing, use another thread of imitation sinew and sew the larger bag ("B") together following the "sewing line" as with "A" (above) using the running stitch.   The top of the pouch is not sewn together as it will provide the place to insert the tobacco pouch, so start sewing at "1" and continue around to "2" as marked.   When this is complete, turn the pouch inside out so that the stitching is hidden inside the bag.

(5)   From the leather, cut eight (8) thongs that are about 1/8" wide and 12" long.   Cut five (5) of these thongs in half so that you have ten (10) thongs that are 6" long and three (3) that are 12" in length.

Figure 2

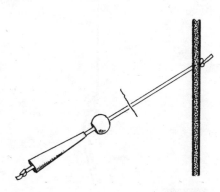

(6)   Using only the ten (10) 6" thongs, make a knot in one end and cut the other end into a point.   As shown in **Figure 2**, pull one thong through each of the holes already made in the front of the pouch so that the knot is hidden inside.   Then, on the pointed end, thread one of the beads and a tin cone on the thong and make a good secure knot.   Pull the tin cone down over this knot.   Do this to each of the ten thongs.

(7)   Now make a small hole through both the front and back of the larger pouch at the two places marked with an "x".   Make a knot at the end of two of the 12" thongs (from above) and, from the back, pull one of these thongs through each of the holes just made.   These thongs will be used to tie the Gage d'More around your neck.   If the pouch will be used to carry a small pipe, slots may be cut from "3" to "4". The stem of the pipe fits down through these.

(8)   The remaining 12" thong may be sewn to the top of the tobacco bag ("A"). Simply tack the thong to the pouch near the top about three (3") inches from the end of the thong.   This, of course, will be wrapped around the top of the small pouch to keep the contents from spilling into the larger bag when stored.

(9)   The *Edging Techniques* that are shown on Page 25 should be self explanatory and any one of them will add a great deal to the appearance of the finished pouch.

HINTS

(A)   If you choose to do any applique or lazy stitch beading on the front or back of the pouch, this should be done before it is sewn together.

(B)   Be sure you remember that the pouch will be turned inside-out after it is finished, so if you want the rough side to show the sewing will be done with the the smooth side exposed, etc.

INDEX

EAGLE'S VIEW BESTSELLERS

❏	The Technique of Porcupine Quill Decoration/Orchard	B00/01	$8.95
❏	In Hardback	B99/01	$15.95
❏	The Technique of North American Indian Beadwork/Smith	B00/02	$9.95
❏	In Hardback	B99/02	$15.95
❏	Techniques of Beading Earrings by Deon DeLange	B00/03	$7.95
❏	More Techniques of Beading Earrings by Deon DeLange	B00/04	$8.95
❏	America's *First* First World War: The French & Indian/Todish	B00/05	$8.95
❏	Crow Indian Beadwork/Wildschut and Ewers	B00/06	$8.95
❏	New Adventures in Beading Earrings by Laura Reid	B00/07	$8.95
❏	North American Indian Burial Customs by Dr. H. C. Yarrow	B00/09	$9.95
❏	Traditional Indian Crafts by Monte Smith	B00/10	$7.95
❏	Traditional Indian Bead & Leather Crafts/ Smith & VanSickle	B00/11	$9.95
❏	Indian Clothing of the Great Lakes: 1740-1840/Hartman	B00/12	$9.95
❏	In Hardback	B99/12	$15.95
❏	Shinin' Trails: A Possibles Bag of Fur Trade Trivia by Legg	B00/13	$7.95
❏	Adventures in Creating Earrings by Laura Reid	B00/14	$9.95
❏	Circle of Power by William F. Higbie	B00/15	$7.95
❏	In Hardback	B99/15	$13.95
❏	Etienne Provost: Man of the Mountains by Jack Tykal	B00/16	$9.95
❏	In Hardback	B99/16	$15.95
❏	A Quillwork Companion by Jean Heinbuch	B00/17	$9.95
❏	In Hardback	B99/17	$15.95
❏	Making Indian Bows & Arrows...The Old Way/Wallentine	B00/18	$9.95
❏	Making Arrows...The Old Way by Doug Wallentine	B00/19	$4.00
❏	Eagle's View Publishing Catalog of Books	B00/99	$1.50

• •

At your local bookstore or use this handy form for ordering:

EAGLE'S VIEW PUBLISHING READERS SERVICE, DEPT TIBLC
6756 North Fork Road - Liberty, Utah 84310

Please send me the above title(s). I am enclosing $_____
(Please add $2.00 per order to cover shipping and handling.) Send check or money
order - no cash or C.O.D.s please.

Ms./Mrs./Mr. _____

Address _____

City/State/Zip Code _____

Prices and availability subject to change without notice. Please allow three to four
weeks for delivery.